IBM DataPower Handbook

Second Edition
Volume II: DataPower Networking

Harley Stenzel

Bill Hines

John Rasmussen

Jim Brennan

Ozair Sheikh

Wild Lake Press

Also Available or Coming Soon! New volumes on Intro/Setup, Development, B2B.

IBM DataPower Appliance Handbook
Second Edition, Volume II

Version 1.0

ISBN: 0990907627

ISBN-13: 978-0990907626

Wild Lake Press

Lake Hopatcong, NJ, USA

www.wildlakepress.com

Please send questions to info@wildlakepress.com and errors/corrections to errata@wildlakepress.com and include the book title and page.

To my wife Emily who encouraged me and worked hard to give me the time I needed for this project; and to my sons Henry and Vincent who are my biggest joys and who tolerated my efforts with remarkably good grace; to my parents gave me a curiosity and a love for learning and language without which this work would not have been possible. —Harley Stenzel

To my mother Carol, who encouraged me to learn, read, and write; to my wonderful, beautiful wife Lori who inspires me and makes me laugh when I need it most; to my children Jennifer, Brittany, and Derek and step-daughters Loriana and Marie; to my sisters Donna and Patty, and the rest of my extended family, who are always there for me; and last but not least, in memory of my beloved father. —Bill Hines

To my mother Marilyn, who has shown me the strength and joy of family and the skills of perseverance; and in memory of my father James, an Officer and a Gentleman, "born on the crest of a wave and rocked in the cradle of the deep." And most of all, to my sons Alex and Nick, who provide me with continuous pride and joy. —John Rasmussen

To my beautiful wife Jennifer and wonderful children Emily, Patrick, and Madison who have all been very patient and supportive of my goals and aspirations even when it meant weekends and late nights away from them. Also to my parents, who always encouraged me to learn and persevere. —Jim Brennan

To my dear wife Khadijah, for her unconditional love and support; and my son Yunus for bringing out the best in me; to my parents who instilled good values and a strong work ethic; and my siblings for their encouragement. —Ozair Sheikh

Contents

Preface

It is with great pleasure that I finally get to introduce the next volume in our series of handbooks on IBM DataPower appliances. We published Volume 1 of this series "DataPower Intro & Setup" in October of 2014, and recently updated it for firmware version 7.2 and added a valuable new chapter on common use cases and deployment scenarios. This new chapter is critical, because many customers are using DataPower for a single purpose, and are not aware of the tremendous amount of capability that it possesses. With this new volume, as well as the upcoming Volume III, which focuses on DataPower Development, and Volume IV on B2B, we are finally getting deep into the technical magic of today's generation of DataPower.

Harley has done a magnificent job in describing DataPower's networking features and configuration, building on the work that Simon Kapadia put into our original first edition hardcover book from 2008. Much has happened in DataPower networking since then, and Harley explores all of the nuances of VLAN, link aggregation, high availability, and much, much more.

Bill Hines, June 21, 2015

They say that change is the only constant. Let's take a moment to remember what the Enterprise Networking world was like back when the original DataPower Handbook was published in 2008.

In 2008, Bill Gates was still at Microsoft, the first ever Andrioid phone was released, and the Summer Olympics were in Bejing. In 2008, it was not unusual to walk into a datacenter with a laptop and a serial cable. VLAN was rarely seen to a host, link aggregation almost never. In 2008, it was still common to see 100Mbps Ethernet used for production traffic.

Now, administrators rarely enter datacenters. VLAN and link aggregation are routinely used to the server, and gigabit Ethernet is ubiquitous. There are new challenges. Virtualization, infrastructure reuse, Everything as a Service. Datacenters are larger, more tightly controlled, and more outsourced. There are more teams, more procedures, and more points of integration.

The world has changed since 2008. Your datacenters have changed. DataPower itself has changed. Some of our advice has likewise changed. But if we take the time to understand the world as it is, we can meet the challenges of today—and those of tomorrow. I hope this volume helps give you the background and the tools you need to meet the challenges you face, now and in the future, even if only some small way.

Harley Stenzel, June 24, 2015

Chapter 1

DataPower as a Network Device

Introduction

In this chapter, you will find everything you need to know to get started with DataPower networking for the developer or administrator. We will introduce the controls offered by the appliance and demonstrate elementary troubleshooting. We'll show straightforward techniques you can use to build good networking habits. This is the place for everyone who uses DataPower to start.

Remember, DataPower exists on the network. All the business value delivered with DataPower depends on the underlying network. If DataPower is the train, then the network is the tracks, and derailment can be difficult and costly to fix. For this reason, it is important that everyone working with the appliance have a certain amount of familiarity with the relationship between DataPower and its network. That is what this chapter provides—the required prerequisites for understanding DataPower's relationship to the network.

Like any host on any network, DataPower requires configuration. The amount of network configuration required varies widely. A personal workstation connected to a simple network has a simple configuration—there simply is not very much to consider. But for an enterprise server there is far more to consider even if the resulting configuration is simple.

In this chapter we'll go through the parts of DataPower networking that are analogous to what one must configure on a workstation. DataPower is capable of integrating into the most complicated of networks. However, as a DataPower administrator or developer the initial pre-deployment network configuration is among the first tasks you perform on a new appliance.

The second goal of this chapter is to help lay a solid foundation for appliance configuration as the appliance moves from a development through test environments and eventually into production. The patterns and habits of development are necessarily promoted through the environments, and it is far easier to start with good habits than to change them after the fact.

DataPower is an Application Layer Proxy Appliance

The DataPower appliance is fundamentally an application layer proxy. It is not a network device—it is an application layer device that has sophisticated network capabilities, but it has more in common with a server daemon than an Ethernet switch.

Nevertheless, DataPower must have IP connectivity in order to fulfill even the simplest of requirements, and simple is where everyone should start.

Configuring Basic Networking

In this section, we will dive into the basic network configuration for DataPower. If you aren't familiar with some of the terms used here, fast forward to the network primer information later in the book and then come back to this part.

To successfully deploy an Ethernet-connected IP host, a few basic pieces of information are required. All of this information comes from the network team, so if you're not sure, you simply have to ask. What you need to know:

What switch and which switch port should I use?

Which port on the appliance should I use? It may be required to provide the Ethernet address of the appliance port to the network team. Some networks require that only a single, known Ethernet address is present on any one switch Ethernet port. If your network has this requirement, the network team will tell you. If your network has this requirement, you cannot substitute a different DataPower interface for the one they have enabled.

TIP— MAC Address/Ethernet Address

The hardware address for the Ethernet implementation of the data link layer is commonly referred to as a Media Access Control, or MAC, address. You will often see the terms "Hardware address," "Ethernet address," and "MAC address" used interchangeably. This is usually valid. Hardware address is more generic and can be used to refer to any technology's hardware addresses. MAC addresses are used by many IEEE 802 specified network technologies. Ethernet addresses are only used for Ethernet networks. Virtual NICs cannot have a "hardware address"—they have no hardware. Nevertheless the hypervisor defines a unique MAC address for each interface of each guest.

What is my hostname?

Should I use DHCP? If yes, omit the remainder of the steps. Note that DHCP can be helpful in some environments, but it is generally unadvised for server use. How will you know the address of your DataPower appliance when you want to send transactions to it? How will you know when its address changes? Nevertheless, DHCP can be useful on virtual appliances, for demonstrations, trainings, and other ad-hoc situations.

What is my IP address and netmask/prefix? Again, these are allocated and assigned by your network administration team.

TIP—IP Address Abstraction

IP addresses on the appliance are the most important artifact to abstract as DataPower moves throughout the development life cycle. This should be the first of only two places that you directly reference IP addresses!

Are there any routes? Is there a default gateway?

What, if any, are the addresses of the DNS, or name servers, I should use?

The single most important thing you can do when deploying a DataPower appliance is to understand all of this, plus the other concepts discussed in this chapter, circulate it widely, and save it for future reference.

DataPower Ethernet Interfaces

DataPower offers a variety of connectivity options, and those options vary based on the model.

Rack-mounted physical appliances such as the XI52, the XG45, and the IDG, or IBM DataPower Gateway series have two non-removable RJ45 gigabit Ethernet ports labeled mgt0 and mgt1 and four to eight removable gigabit ports beginning with eth10. They also have two 10-gigabit Ethernet SFP+ labeled eth20 and eth21.

Virtual Edition appliances as initially deployed have four "Ethernet" interfaces labeled eth0 through eth3. Note that the Ethernet interfaces that are available depend on the hypervisor configuration, and can be changed after deployment.

Be sure to match the virtual Ethernet type of any changed interfaces to the same type as was originally present. So on VMWare when the original deployment use the "vmxnet3" driver, ensure that the same driver is used after changing the hypervisor configuration. This might require hand-editing the ".vmx" file!

Blade form factor appliances (XI50B and XI50z) have two 1-gigabit Ethernet interfaces named eth1 and eth2. They have those names because they are associated with the BladeCenter chassis IO bays 1 and 2 respectively. The XI50B and XI50z additionally have two 10-gigabit Ethernet interfaces named eth7 and eth9 because they are associated with the BladeCenter chassis high-speed IO bays 7 and 9 respectively. Bladecenter Management is a topic unto itself. If you find yourself working with the XI50B and are unfamiliar with the administration of the chassis, be sure to involve the team with that responsibility. It is a specialty that, like network administration or DataPower administration, involves a great deal of domain knowledge.

Ethernet Interface Configuration Settings

The Ethernet Interface configuration panel is located in the default domain. In the WebGUI, it is under Network→Interface→Ethernet Interface. From that screen, select the single Ethernet interface that you want to configure.

Now, the first time you configure an appliance, you will have to use the CLI over the serial console. The principles are the same and the information required is the same, but the syntax is of course different. Not to worry, we have CLI examples farther on in this chapter. The first volume in this book series, DataPower Handbook, Second Edition, Volume 1: Intro & Setup also covers initial configuration.

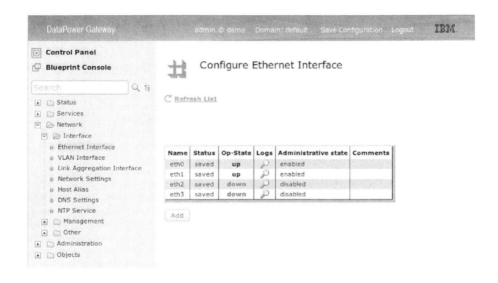

Figure 1-1 Configure Ethernet Interface

Figure 1-1 shows the navigation to the Configure Ethernet Interface configuration screen along with the list of Ethernet Interfaces on an IBM DataPower Gateway (IDG) Virtual appliance.

Figure 1-2 shows the Configure Ethernet Interface screen for Ethernet eth0 on an IDG Virtual appliance. The Ethernet interface configuration screen has three tabs: Main, Standby Control, and Advanced. Only the Main tab is routinely required in order to configure an appliance for basic connectivity. Simply fill in the values in the correct fields and click on the Apply button.

Configure Ethernet Interface

Main   Standby control   Advanced

Ethernet Interface: eth0 [up]

Cancel   Delete   Undo

Export | View Log | View Status | Help
Start packet capture | Stop packet capture | Disable hardware offload | Yield standby

Basic configuration

Administrative state
◉ enabled ○ disabled

Comments

IP address configuration mode
☑ Static
☐ DHCP
☐ SLAAC

Enable for link aggregation
○ on ◉ off

IP addressing

Primary IP Address
192.168.116.200/24

Secondary Addresses
{empty}

[   ] add

IP routing

Default IPv4 gateway
192.168.116.2   Ping Remote

Default IPv6 gateway
Ping Remote

Static routes

Destination	Next-hop router	Metric
{empty}		
		Add

Figure 1-2 Ethernet eth0 configuration

TIP—Network Properties

Most of the properties we have to configure are not actually Ethernet at all. Most network interface configuration, no matter the kind of network interface, is about configuring the IP layer. Hence, all IP configurations are identical for

Ethernet, VLAN, and link aggregation interfaces that we'll discuss more in Chapter 2, "Advanced DataPower Networking."

■ ▬ ▬ ▬ ▬ ▬ ▬ ▬ ▬ ▬ ▬

Basic Configuration Section

Let's have a look at the configurable properties in the Basic Configuration Section. "Administrative state" can be either enabled or disabled. Set this field to enabled only on interfaces that you are using. You should disable interfaces that are not otherwise configured or not in use.

The "Comments" field is not required, but it is a good idea to include information like the intended purpose of the interface and the switch port the interface is physically connected to. It is a free-form text field.

"IP address configuration mode" is a tri-state variable that controls the way the interface receives its IP layer configuration. It can be either Static, DHCP, or SLAAC. "Static" is both the default and the most common option. With Static addressing, you configure the addresses and routes directly on the configuration screen. The other options are for automatic addressing. With DHCP the interface will try to discover its address from a DHCP server. SLAAC is IPv6 auto-configuration and is not commonly used. IP Addresses and IP routes can only be specified when IP address configuration mode is Static.

"Enable for link aggregation" is either ON or OFF. Leave it off for now—it's not part of a simple network configuration! As long as link aggregation is off, every other setting on this tab relates to configuring IP.

IP Addressing Section

"Primary IP Address" is the IP address provided by the network team. It will have the subnet information imbedded and is usually written in the form 1.2.3.4/24, where the address is 1.2.3.4 and the subnet prefix length is 24. Be sure to supply the address with the prefix everywhere you configure an IP address on an interface!

TIP—CIDR Notation

CIDR notation, pronounced "cider," is a way of expressing variable length subnet masks by simply stating the number of masking bits. It is usually shown by adding an IP address with the suffix / and the number—for instance the 10.48.245.153/23 is equivalent to 10.48.245.153 with subnet mask 255.255.254.0. The number after the / is called the "prefix" or "prefix length."

"Secondary IP Addresses" are for any additional IP addresses that should be on the interface and that are part of the same network. If you have secondary addresses, add them here.

Secondary addresses have many uses, among them is to allow a development or test environment where there may be only one network interface present to be functionally equivalent to a production device. A production device might have several addresses on different networks configured on different DataPower interfaces. A device in lower dev/test environments, may have the same number of addresses, but they all may be on the same interface!

It is still important that all the IP addresses configured on the interface be assigned to the appliance, but if one can have multiple addresses assigned on the same network it sets the stage for far easier transitions between environments.

This is one of the two places where IP addresses must be directly configured. The other is the "Host Alias." It is a best practice to configure an each IP address on the appliance with a Host Alias and to use that host alias elsewhere in the appliance configuration to refer to the local address.

When IP addresses are added to the interface configuration, they can be either IPv4 or IPv6. Nearly every DataPower service supports IPv4 or IPv6 addresses. When host aliases are used to abstract away the address from the name, the host alias itself can be either IPv4 or IPv6.

TIP— IP v4/v6 Notation

IPv4 addresses are written in "dotted-quad" notation, with four 8-bit decimal numbers separated by the "." character. IPv6 addresses look different—they are written in groups of 16-bit hexadecimal characters separated by ":". Any one consecutive group that are all 0's are shortened to "::".

IP Routing Section

"Default IPv4 gateway" and/or "Default IPv6 gateway" must be configured only when one exists for this network. If one was not provided by the networking team, then you should not have one! Remember, a default route is a sign that says "The world is over there." It's a good sign to have, but only if it really is true. An appliance that should not access the Internet should probably not have a default gateway.

TIP—Configuring Multiple Interfaces

If you are connecting more than one of DataPower's interfaces, you owe it to yourself to work through the Advanced DataPower Networking chapter and to have a very comfortable relationship with your network architecture and administration teams!

"Static Routes" are the general case routes, and are more flexible than default routes. Your network team might give you a route like 10.0.0.0/8 via 10.48.244.1. This route says that "all the rest of the 10-dot network is over there," implying that the rest of the Internet is not.

TIP—Default Gateways

Beware signs of trouble such as having more than one default gateway on an appliance or adding routes for single hosts to override standard routing. These are indications that a serious discussion with the network architecture team is in order. Ignoring these signs of trouble is a good way to experience an outage!

Other Interface Configuration

The Standby Control tab is used for network-based hot-standby and fail-over, and should not be considered in the simple deployment scenario. It is only usable when static IP configuration is enabled—it can't be used with DHCP.

The Advanced tab has a few properties that may be specified by your network administration team. It is rare that settings on the advanced tab need to be changed.

"MTU," or Maximum Transmit Unit. The default is 1500, which is standard for Ethernet. Another common setting is 9000, used with Ethernet jumbo frames.

"MAC Addresses" provides a way to set the Ethernet address. Be careful, if more than one Ethernet station on the same network have the same MAC address, it is likely that neither station will have connectivity, and there may be collateral damage too! This setting is most often used when the switch is configured to only permit a single known MAC address and the appliance is a replacement. In this case, you would configure the old appliance's MAC address onto the replacement appliance. This will be discussed in more detail later in this volume.

"Physical Mode" is nearly always auto. Sometimes switches are configured to only offer a single mode. In these cases, the appliance sometimes has to be configured that way too. It is best to try auto first and make a change only at the request of the switch owner.

Configuring Ethernet Interface via the Command Line

Network configuration is more often done from the command line than other forms of configuration. The simple reason is– for many types of network devices, there may not be a way to use another form of configuration! In order to use the WebGUI, initial network configuration must be performed either on the CLI or in the initial install wizard.

An example of how configuring a DataPower Virtual Edition eth0 interface from the DataPower command line is in Listing 1-1. This sort of configuration would be enough to give the appliance connectivity for further configuration through the WebGUI.

The DataPower CLI is a command language similar to other networking products, and will be familiar to network administrators.

Listing 1-1 CLI Ethernet configuration

```
top; co;
ethernet eth0
  ip-address 10.48.245.153/23
  ipv4-default-gateway 10.48.244.1
exit
write mem
```

Ethernet Configuration Summary

The goal is proper integration with the existing network, and there are facts about the network that are simply not discoverable. One must be told what these values should be. The surest way to avoid trouble is to ask questions early and often, and the surest way to get into trouble is to change settings without a thorough understanding of how the appliance is integrating with and operating in the network.

Other Network Settings

In addition to the network interface configuration, there are other network-related settings that are applicable even with basic networking.

Like the interface configuration, these settings vary from host to host or environment to environment.

Configure Name Servers

Most likely you will have one or two DNS name servers. Configure these as specified by your network administration team. Note that these are expected to be different for different network environments—be sure to use the ones that are correct for where your appliance is located.

TIP—Adding Name Servers and Search Domains

Less is more when it comes to name servers and search domains. Adding additional name servers and search domains dramatically increases the amount of time it takes to resolve a name under failure. What happens when your production appliance cannot resolve names? What strategies do you have to mitigate this failure? For the answers to these questions and more, see Chapter 2, "DataPower Advanced Networking!"

As a general rule, two name servers and a single search domain is a good place to start.

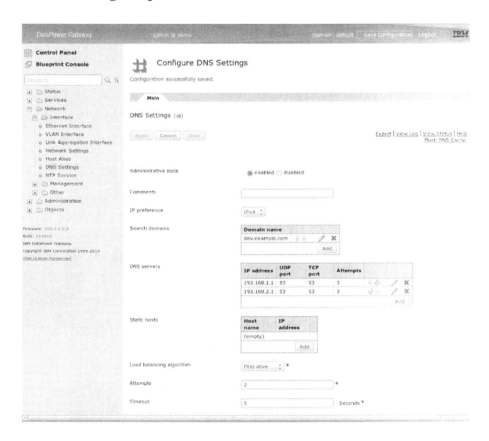

Figure 1-3 Configure DNS Settings

The DNS configuration object also provides "Static Hosts." These are the equivalent of a "/etc/hosts" file, where an administrator can manually configure names for an IP address that overrides DNS. This provides another way to abstract away names from IP addresses in a more fine-grained fashion. Be careful when overriding DNS! It can be confusing when a name has a different address but only on one host.

Overall, the combination of name servers, search domains, and static hosts provides all the tools necessary to allow DataPower services to move from environment to environment without changes to the other services in the DataPower configuration. Consider the following scenario:

As developers, we know that we need to use DataPower to access an LDAP server. We have access to a preproduction version of that LDAP server that we will use to develop and unit test my DataPower configuration. However, that LDAP server is running on another development system, and has a name that is less than useful. We know that when our service is eventually promoted to production, the LDAP server is named "ldap.<datacenter-id>.example.com," because there is a cluster running in each datacenter.

It would be counterproductive to have my unhelpfully named development LDAP server's name appear in the service configuration that will be promoted. What to do?

Just call it "ldap" in the DataPower service configuration, and add a Static Host in the DataPower DNS configuration that associates the name "ldap" with the IP address of the development LDAP server with the unhelpful name.

Later, in the final preproduction and production environments, you have several choices of how to associate "ldap" with the IP address of the LDAP server in the target environment.

It could use the same strategy used in development—a static host. It could use the search domain to tell the difference. Or it could use the set of name servers defined to tell the difference. For our purposes now, this question does not matter. What is important is that the target server is abstracted away from the service objects and into the DNS configuration.

There are a few other things to keep in mind when thinking about a strategy of how to use the same name for different hosts under different circumstances.

First, remember that the static hosts are appliance wide—the DNS configuration object only exists in the default domain. It only makes sense to use the static host as the abstraction point when new LDAP is applicable to every service in every domain on the appliance. The appliance may be a virtual appliance and may be only used by one developer. If this is the case, then the administrator and developer are the same person and a static host may make a great deal of sense. But if the development appliance is shared and only one developer has to use the "new LDAP," a static host change could help one user and hurt another.

The other thing to keep in mind is that there are other ways to manage what changes in different environments. DataPower offers deployment policies for this reason. Deployment policies will be discussed in a later volume in this series.

TIP— To FQDN or Not, That is the Question

To FQDN or not, that is the question? A FQDN, or Fully Qualified Domain Name, is the combination of a host name plus its domain. So if the hostname is "myhost" and the domain is "dev.example.com," the FQDN is "myhost.dev.example.com". Since the FQDN is the second most specific way of referring to an IP host (second only to its IP address), FQDNs should not generally be used in portable configuration because by definition portable configuration is expected to use different hosts at different stages in the life cycle of the service.

Expect that each appliance in the same role and location have the same DNS configuration.

Listing 1-2 Configuring DNS in the CLI

```
top; co
dns
   name-server 10.48.20.10
   name-server 10.48.21.10
   search-domain dev.example.com
   static-host ldap 10.48.245.160
exit
```

Host Alias

Host Aliases are similar to static hosts except they are used for the appliance's own IP addresses. Whereas static hosts should be used to refer hosts that the appliance must contact in the course of processing transactions, host aliases are used to abstract the IP address that is bound to the service.

INFO— Host Aliases are NOT DNS Static Hosts!

Host Aliases are NOT DNS Static Hosts! A Host Alias is for IP addresses local to the appliance. A Static Host is for IP addresses that you connect to from the appliance.

Consider the scenario where the final deployment will have three IP addresses, one for appliance management, one for Internet-facing traffic with its own SSL cert, and one for internal traffic, also with its own SSL cert.

As a developer or administrator you may know this is the end goal, but you still might only have one network interface and you may only have one IP address. How can you create configuration that is not sensitive to the lack of similarity between your environment and the target environment?

This is the purpose of host aliases.

In this example, the DataPower administrator would create three different host aliases called "Internet," "internal," and "management" as seen in Figure 1-4 and Figure 1-5.

Then the DataPower developers and administrators would make use of the host aliases. For any Internet-facing service configuration the developer would use the "Internet" host alias in the "Local address" field. Similarly, on all internal-facing services he would use the "Internal" host alias, and for services like ssh, xml-mgmt, and web-mgmt, the DataPower administrator would use the "management" host alias. Figure 1-6 shows DataPower ssh using the management host alias. Notice that you can use the Select Alias button to choose the appropriate alias! Not only is it better in the long run to use host aliases, it can be easier too.

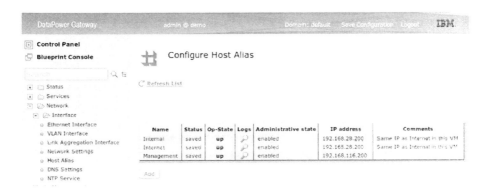

Figure 1-4 Configure Host Alias screen with host alias Internet, Internal, and management

Figure 1-5 Configure Host Alias for the Internet host alias.

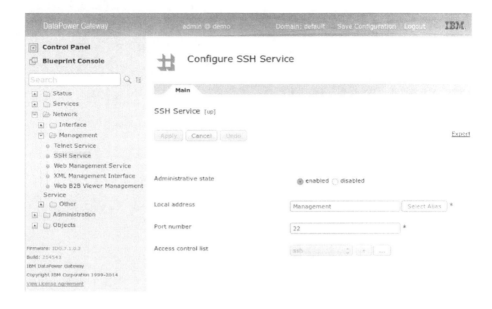

Figure 1-6 SSH using the management host alias

Avoid defining a host alias for every service present in the final configuration. Instead, use a host alias for each logical role. The same of host aliases should be consistent in development, test, pre-production, and production environments. Having a host alias for each logical role does not mean you have to have an IP address for each logical role! Several host aliases can have the same IP address, so even if you guess wrong about what will be separated, it's better to have too much separation than too little—just don't go overboard.

This approach may seem overly complicated when one is only considering a single appliance, but DataPower services are rarely confined to a single appliance. They are developed in one place, tested in several others, and deployed in many others. By using host aliases in this way, each appliance can have its own host aliases and every other part of the IP configuration can be shared.

Hostname and other System Settings

The DataPower appliance also has a number of network-related settings in System Settings.

Configure the appliance name in Administration, System Settings. The appliance name is equivalent to the hostname on a Windows, OSX, Linux, or Unix system It should be unique and it should correspond to the name of the management IP address if possible. Set it as seen in in Figure 1-7.

Additionally, the Location field is helpful in identifying where this appliance resides.

TIP— Using the Location Light

When looking for a particular rack-mounted appliance, the Location field should tell you everything you need to know. But if it does not, you can use the location light to help find the appliance. Just turn it on in the GUI and then look for the appliance that has it lit up. The location light can help seal the deal—just don't forget to turn it off when you're done.

For physical appliances, it should identify the datacenter, room, rack, rack location, and any special instructions. For instance—"Mailing   address. Floor/Room/Isle/Column/Cabinet/U. Terminal server 8/21"

For blade form factor based appliances, be sure to also include the BladeCenter chassis identification information and the slot within the chassis. You'll also want to know how to access the management module for the chassis.

If the appliance is virtual, you'll want to know how to access the hypervisor console. Overall though, the general advice is to have enough information in the location field to be able to find the appliance and administer it in case of emergency.

Figure 1-7 System Settings from an IDG Virtual Appliance with name, location, and contact set.

Lights-Out Management

Every DataPower appliance should have a way that the appliance can be remotely managed that does not depend on the appliance's network stack. Traditionally, the serial console was the only method offered, and appliances were deployed either with a serial connection to a terminal server to provide lights-out or out-of-band management, but often the strategy was to send someone to the data center with a laptop. The former strategy requires additional hardware and infrastructure; the latter is inconvenient and increasingly unpalatable.

Fortunately, recent generations of the rack-mounted form factor appliance offer a better strategy—they include an integrated management card based on the IPMI (Integrated Platform Management Interface) specification. With this, one can perform a broad range of management tasks including powering the appliance on or off and accessing the serial console—all done remotely and all available even when the power to the appliance is turned off. All this is configured via the IPMI LAN Channel.

Similar function is available on other form factors, but it is delivered in a different way. For virtual, the hypervisor has the role of power control and console access. For blade, the BladeCenter management module delivers this capability.

To configure IPMI, follow the steps in Listing 1-3.

Listing 1-3: Configure DataPower IPMI for remote serial and power control.

```
top; co
ipmi-user admin
  reset
  password mysupersecretpassword
exit
ipmi-lan-channel mgt0
  reset
  maximum-channel-privilege-level operator
```

```
allowed-user admin operator on 0
ip address 10.48.245.160/24
ip default-gateway 10.48.245.1
exit
```

After the management module is configured, it can be accessed with any IPMI compliant client such as "ipmitool." You can find ipmitool at http://sourceforge.net/projects/ipmitool/, it is a BSD-licensed open source IPMI client.

Access the serial console: ipmitool -I lanplus -H 10.48.245.160 -U admin -L operator sol activate

Power off the appliance: ipmitool -I lanplus -H 10.48.245.160 -U admin -L operator chassis power off

Power on the appliance: ipmitool -I lanplus -H 10.48.245.160 -U admin -L operator chassis power on

Note that the management board is logically a totally different Ethernet station that shares a port with mgt0. It has its own Ethernet address and it requires its own IP address—it is truly its own dedicated device. Also it can only have a default gateway so mgt0 must never be used as an Internet-facing network interface.

Figure 1-8 shows the relationship on the DataPower Ethernet port labeled mgt0. The same figure shows both the physical cabling and the logical relationship between the switch port, the DataPower mgt0 Ethernet interface, and the IPMI LAN channel on mgt0. As you can see, the IPMI LAN channel really is its own Ethernet station.

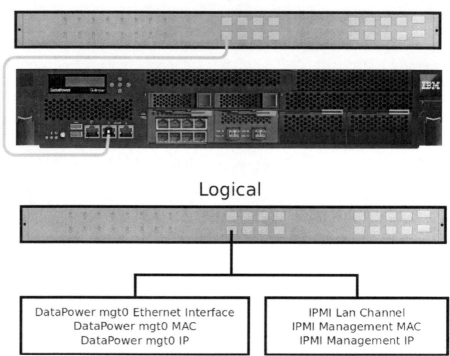

Figure 1-8 DataPower mgt0 port cabling vs Ethernet mgt0 and Lan Channel configuration

WARNING— Mgt0 Interface Security

Because of IPMI, never connect mgt0 to a network unless it is a trusted management network. To do otherwise could expose IPMI to people and computers to which it should not be exposed.

No matter how lights-out or out-of-band management is delivered, each deployment needs a strategy. Who can access the management console? Under what circumstances? With what permissions / passwords? Via what networks? These questions apply equally to IPMI, Management Modules, or Hypervisors.

Configuration Conclusion

There are two basic goals in configuring a DataPower appliance: First, one must achieve simple Ethernet connectivity—Ethernet because it is the simplest, and connectivity because without that, the appliance is useless.

The second and more important goal of the concepts described in this section is the understanding of the relationships between IP addresses, hostnames, host aliases, static hosts, and how they relate to DataPower services and appliance life cycle.

IP addresses assigned to the appliance should be used directly in only two places: in IP interface configuration and as host aliases. Care must be taken to ensure that IP addresses are not used elsewhere in the appliance configuration—not in stylesheets, not in gateway script, and not directly on the configuration panels. Don't allow incorrectly-scoped configuration to exist where it does not belong!

Each appliance will have one or more interface and host aliases configuration. Each appliance that shares a role and zone will share its DNS and static host configuration. Each service should use a host alias as its "listen address" or front-side address.

Choose host aliases wisely, for it is easier to have different host aliases that use the same address than it is to have services that must later be split apart to use different host aliases. Host aliases are for addresses on the appliance itself—not for external servers (those go in the Static Hosts configuration area).

Have a strategy in mind for DNS and static hosts to effectively distinguish between hosts the appliance communicates with when the configuration is placed in different zones.

Ensure that services do not accidentally include artifacts from one network that one development appliance uses, or those could unintentionally find their way into production appliance configurations.

Have a lights-out or out-of-band management strategy for each appliance in each zone. It might be as simple as "someone walks to the lab" or it might require an operations team have remote access to an appliance where physical access is extremely limited.

Verifying and Troubleshooting Network Configuration

After networking is configured on an appliance, the logical next step is to verify that it is working as expected. Again, this process is not so different for DataPower than compared to other network devices, but the particulars do vary.

The first way to verify is to check status. One only needs to look at the large list of entries in the WebGUI under Status, IP-

Network as seen in Figure 1-9 to get a sense of the breadth. In this section we'll highlight a few of the most helpful tips for verifying that DataPower's networking facilities are properly configured for its network. DataPower has its own way to look at the route table, the interface settings, ARP table, etc. Remember that network troubleshooting is often done when the WebGUI is inaccessible, so we'll focus on the CLI techniques.

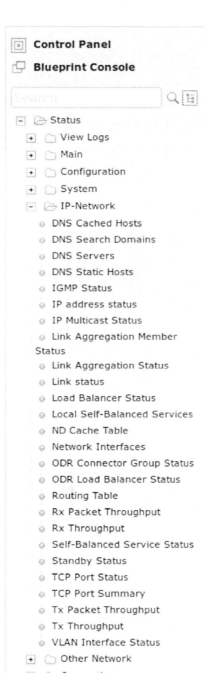

Figure 1-9 IP-Network Status

The second way is to test it out. This can be done either from DataPower itself or from the client / server connecting to DataPower. DataPower has its own way to ping another host and to establish a TCP connection with a specific port.

The combination of the two techniques are usually enough to determine the problem, so that's what we'll focus on here. But if that's not enough there are still other ways, ranging from detailed log analysis to packet capture. But if the networking configuration is straightforward (and it should be!) status and probing will suffice.

Status

Status reflects what the appliance is actually doing. Of course we expect the actual results to be consistent with what we ordered, and likely expect a bit of extra detail. That is exactly what status provides. If the configuration is the online order to your favorite online store, the status is the moment when you open the box and behold the glory of your new widget.

On the WebGUI, status is grouped together under the "Status" section of the navigation panel on the left, as shown in Figure 1-9.

Status vs Configuration in the CLI

In the command-line interface, the "show" command will show both config and status. If the "show" argument is the same as a config noun, then "show" will display configuration. For instance, to configure Ethernet, we use the command "top; co; ethernet eth10; . . .". To display the configuration for Ethernet, the command "show ethernet" suffices.

Another way to tell the difference between configuration and status is by the output format. Configuration always has the following command format as its first line:

<command>: <object-name> [<status>]

An Ethernet example:

ethernet: eth3 [up]

Whenever you are looking at a "show" command in the CLI, be sure you know if it is for configuration or for status. That's how you can know if it's what you asked for or what is actually happening.

Link Status

If the appliance does not have connectivity on an interface, or appears to have poor connectivity, the link status is the place to start. It is "show link" on the CLI. Figures 1-10 and 1-11 show the CLI and WebGUI versions of Link Status.

```
idg# show link

Name      ifIndex  Status    Mode          Type      MTU    Aggregate interface  Link address
------    -------  -------   ----------    --------   ----   -------------------  ----------------
lo        1        ok        none          Other      16436                       00:00:00:00:00:00
eth0      5        ok        10GBASE-KX4   Ethernet   1500                        00:0c:29:9a:18:e5
eth1      6        ok        10GBASE-KX4   Ethernet   1500                        00:0c:29:9a:18:ef
eth2      7        no-link   none          Ethernet   1500                        00:0c:29:9a:18:f9
eth3      8        no-link   none          Ethernet   1500                        00:0c:29:9a:18:03
gre0      2        no-link   none          Other      1476                        00:00:00:00:00:00
sit0      3        no-link   none          Other      1480                        00:00:00:00:00:00
ip6tnl0   4        no-link   none          Other      1460                        00:00:00:00:00:00
```

Figure 1-10 CLI show link

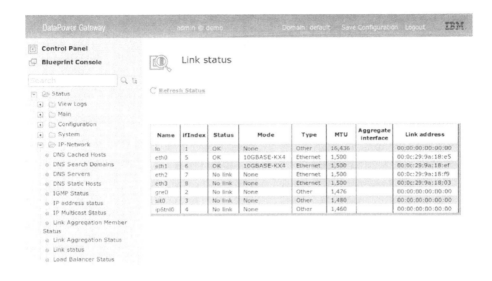

Figure 1-11 WebGUI Link Status

For no connectivity, note the "status" column. If it indicates no-link, then correct the problem. It could be a bad or missing cable, unseated connection, disabled switch port, or any number of things that prevent the appliance from establishing an Ethernet link. In this case, eth2 and eth3 are do not have link because they are admin disabled. See Figure 1-1. It shows both eth2 and eth3 are Op-State down and Administrative state disabled.

Check the "Mode." It should show the speed you expect— the maximum shared speed of the appliance's Ethernet interface and the upstream switch port. If there is marginal connectivity, mismatched mode is often the issue– especially if the mode shows "HD" or half-duplex. In rare cases, it may be necessary to configure the switch or the appliance such that they negotiate speed and duplex correctly.

Lastly, there are links present that you may not recognize. Not to worry, they are present for DataPower capabilities that are not directly configurable. Nevertheless, they are still network interfaces. Examples from Figure 1-10 and Figure 1-11 include lo, gre0, sit0, and ip6tnl0. The lo interface is loopback. The sit0 interface is an IPv6 artifact, and the remainder are present for DataPower's Sysplex Distributor integration. But don't worry about them too much—you probably won't need or use them.

IP Address Status

The IP Address shows every IP address present on DataPower's network stack. You should find every address you configured in that list, and some you didn't. It is "show ipaddress" on the CLI as seen in Figure 1-12 and Figure 1-13.

Expect to see the primary address for each network interface you configured, along with the network interface it is configured on and the prefix length. Also expect to see built-in addresses like 127.0.0.1 on interface "lo".

There are other examples of ways one might have additional IP addresses configured on the appliance's stack, such as Standby Control which uses interfaces with a "-vip" suffix (more on that later) or the rarely-used Sysplex Distributor integration.

What you won't find is rows for network interfaces that do not have any IP addresses!

When checking the IP address status, be sure you find each IP address you expect to have on the system and that it has the correct prefix length and is on the correct interface.

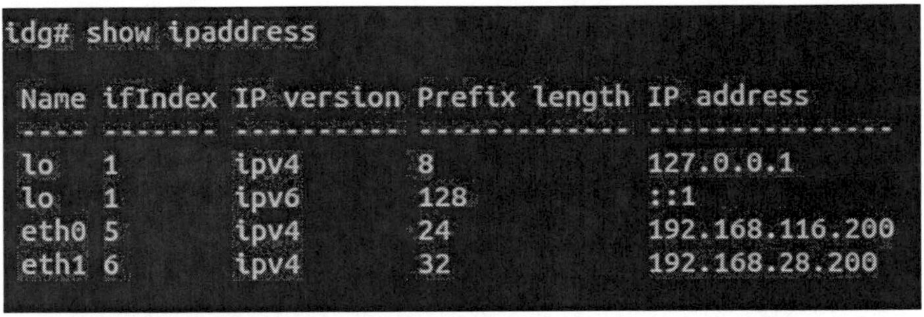
idg# show ipaddress
Name ifIndex IP version Prefix length IP address
lo 1 ipv4 8 127.0.0.1
lo 1 ipv6 128 ::1
eth0 5 ipv4 24 192.168.116.200
eth1 6 ipv4 32 192.168.28.200

Figure 1-12 CLI show ipaddress from and IDG Virtual Appliance

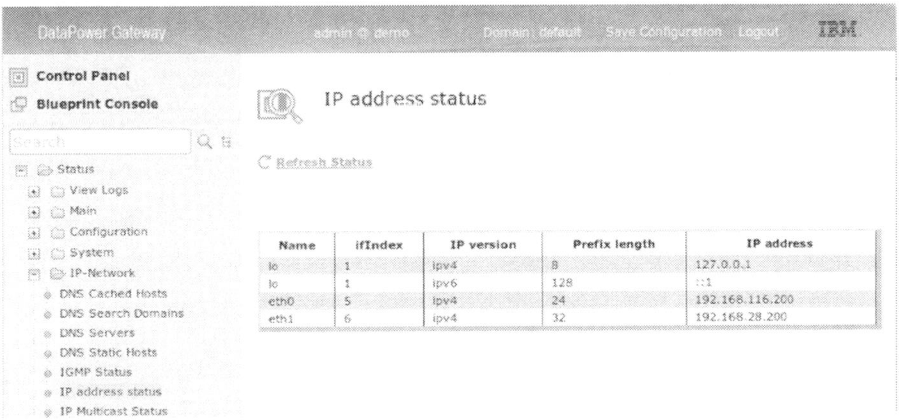
DataPower Gateway
admin @ demo
Domain: default
Save Configuration
Logout
IBM
Control Panel
Blueprint Console
Search
Status
View Logs
Main
Configuration
System
IP-Network
DNS Cached Hosts
DNS Search Domains
DNS Servers
DNS Static Hosts
IGMP Status
IP address status
IP Multicast Status
IP address status
Refresh Status
Name ifIndex IP version Prefix length IP address
lo 1 ipv4 8 127.0.0.1
lo 1 ipv6 128 ::1
eth0 5 ipv4 24 192.168.116.200
eth1 6 ipv4 32 192.168.28.200

Figure 1-13 WebGUI IP Address Status from an IDG Virtual Appliance.

IP Route Status

The IP Route status provider, which is “show route” on the CLI, is similar to Windows' “route print” command or the *nix “route” command provides a display of the routes present on the appliance.

Verify that every route is expected based on the configuration supplied.

A Default gateway, whether directly configured or acquired from DHCP appears as a route to 0.0.0.0/0 with a next-hop. The first route in Figures 1-14 and 1-15 is the default route.

Implied subnet routes are always present for every directly-connected subnet. There will be one for each subnet defined on each interface. These are routes that are created automatically from the IP address on each interface. In Figures 1-14 and 1-15, every route except the default gateway is an implied subnet route.

Static routes will also appear—ensure that every static route is accounted for by matching its destination, prefix, interface, next-hop, and metric to the configured values. Also ensure that all configured values are observed in status. The example configuration does not have any static routes other than the default gateways. This is not uncommon for a developer using IDG Virtual Edition on their laptop.

The most common way a routing problem presents itself is that some destinations can be reached and others cannot. Unfortunately, that symptom is not very specific—while it could indicate a routing problem, it could also indicate a firewall or hostname problem, as the firewall could be blocking the request and the attempt to connect to the wrong host or IP address can present in a similar manner.

```
idg# show route

IP version Destination    Prefix length Interface type Interface Next hop version Next hop          Metric
---------- -----------    ------------- -------------- --------- ---------------- --------          ------
ipv4       0.0.0.0        0             Ethernet       eth0      ipv4             192.168.116.2 200
ipv4       192.168.116.0  24            Ethernet       eth0      ipv4             0.0.0.0           0
ipv6       fe80::         64            Ethernet       eth0      ipv6             ::                256
ipv6       fe80::         64            Ethernet       eth1      ipv6             ::                256
```

Figure 1-14 CLI show route from an IDG Virtual Appliance

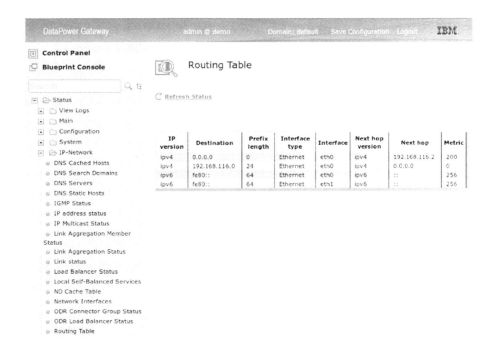

IP version	Destination	Prefix length	Interface type	Interface	Next hop version	Next hop	Metric
ipv4	0.0.0.0	0	Ethernet	eth0	ipv4	192.168.116.2	200
ipv4	192.168.116.0	24	Ethernet	eth0	ipv4	0.0.0.0	0
ipv6	fe80::	64	Ethernet	eth0	ipv6	::	256
ipv6	fe80::	64	Ethernet	eth1	ipv6	::	256

Figure 1-15 WebGUI Routing Table from an IDG Virtual Appliance.

Network Interface Status

Network Interface status shows every network interface on the appliance plus critical counters such as receive and transmit bytes, packets, errors, and drops. It is equivalent to the "show network-interface" in the command-line interface. Figure 1-16 and Figure 1-17 show the network interface status on the CLI and WebGui respectively.

If any of the error counts are increasing, check the mode, swap out the cable, and if the problem persists engage your network team. It is not uncommon for there to be short bursts of such errors as a cable is connected or disconnected, so no need to worry if you can attribute the errors to known events.

Receive and transmit counters are helpful for identifying which interfaces are actually being used and its purpose.

For all the counters, it is helpful to know how they are changing over time. For that, there is no substitute for taking snapshots a known time period apart.

TIP— Using Show Time for Status Results

On the command-line, use "show time; show network-interface," then save the result, and issue the same command again a bit later. That way, you'll have the time basis for each status result.

Figure 1-16 CLI show network-interface from an IDG Virtual Appliance

Figure 1-17 WebGUI Network Interfaces from an IDG Virtual Appliance.

TCP Port Status

The TCP Port Status is the equivalent of a "netstat -an" on a distributed platform. In DataPower CLI, it is "show tcp". It lists the TCP sockets on a given device, what state they are in, what the source and destination addresses and ports are, and so on. If you look for just the sockets that are in "listen" state, you can see all the services that are active on a device, which domain they are in, and what IP address they are bound to.

The most important use of this screen is to check which services are listening on which ports. There can only be a single TCP service (such as an XML Firewall or a Front Side Handler) listening on a given IP address and port combination; if due to a misconfiguration or miscommunication, two services have been configured to listen on the same IP address and port, only the first one that tries to bind will be able to start. Using the TCP port status screen, if a service is down we can easily check to see whether another service is using its IP address and port combination, to see whether that is the reason the service didn't start.

If the local IP address appears as "0.0.0.0" or "::" then the service listening on the port is not bind-specific. This indicates that the service was not configured to use the host alias. While this is of course permitted, it means that the configuration of the service maybe inappropriate for some environments. If the service is the WebGUI, then you may be exposing the WebGUI to the Internet. That would be most inappropriate.

Speaking of host aliases, keep in mind that the TCP status provider shows the actual addresses, not the host alias. In Figures 1-18 and 1-19, you can see that local port 22 is in listen state on IP address 192.168.116.200. But looking back at Figure 1-6 recall that we used the Management host alias when configuring the SSH service. Figure 1-4 shows that the Management host alias is 192.168.116.200.

If there are a large number of time-wait connections with an http or https listening port, that indicates there is a HTTP-layer protocol problem between the client and DataPower that caused DataPower to routinely close its side of the connection first. In TCP, we expect the client to normally close() before the server. Note that this only applies when the local address is a HTTP or HTTPS listener. DataPower also acts as a HTTP or HTTPS client, and in those cases we expect the TCP connection to end up in time-wait.

If TCP ports are stuck in syn-sent or syn-received it likely means that no packets can make it from DataPower to the remote address and port combination, probably because of a routing configuration problem, a firewall, or an incorrect remote IP address.

```
idg(config)# show tcp

local address              remote address              state
-------------              --------------              -----
127.0.0.1:31338            127.0.0.1:63503             established
127.0.0.1:31370            127.0.0.1:63503             established
192.168.116.200:22         0.0.0.0:0                   listen
192.168.116.200:22         192.168.116.1:51110         established
192.168.116.200:5550       0.0.0.0:0                   listen
192.168.116.200:9090       0.0.0.0:0                   listen
192.168.116.200:9090       192.168.116.1:57397         established
192.168.116.200:9090       192.168.116.1:57398         established
192.168.116.200:9090       192.168.116.1:57399         established
192.168.116.200:9090       192.168.116.1:57400         established
192.168.116.200:9090       192.168.116.1:57401         established
192.168.116.200:9090       192.168.116.1:57402         established

  established: 9
     syn-sent: 0
 syn-received: 0
   fin-wait-1: 0
   fin-wait-2: 0
    time-wait: 0
       closed: 0
   close-wait: 0
     last-ack: 0
       listen: 3
      closing: 0
```

Figure 1-18 show tcp from an IDG Virtual Appliance.

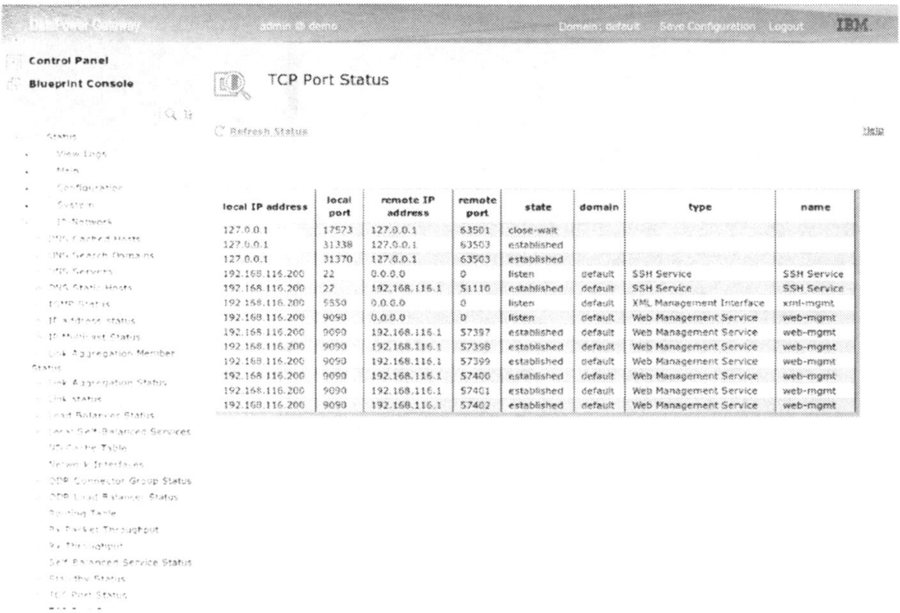

Figure 1-19 TCP Port Status from an IDG Virtual Appliance.

ARP Table

The Address Resolution Protocol (ARP) resolves IP addresses to physical Ethernet addresses. Like other Ethernet stations on an IP network, the appliance maintains an ARP cache, and you can list the current cache of nodes for which ARP has completed in the ARP table, like "arp -a" on distributed platforms. The ARP table can be displayed using the "show netarp" command in the CLI as shown in Figure 1-20.

The device's ARP cache contains the hardware addresses of all the Ethernet stations in the local broadcast domain that the appliance is in direct communication. Put another way, only IP addresses in a local subnet are present. Frequently, the arp cache is quite small since most IP traffic tranmits via a router,

and the arp cache only has a single entry for all of that traffic—
that of the router.

You should expect to see entries for each of your routers,
assuming you have sent traffic via that router recently. You
should also see entries for other IP hosts on your subnet which
you have recently communicated.

This is a command that is only available on the CLI. There
is no WebGUI equivalent.

```
idg# show netarp

IP address     MAC address               Interface Interface Type VLAN
-------------- ------------------------- --------- -------------- ----
192.168.116.1 00:50:56:c0:00:08 eth0             Ethernet
192.168.116.2 00:50:56:e8:93:2a eth0             Ethernet
```

Figure 1-20 CLI show netarp

Tests from DataPower

For testing, diagnosing, and debugging connectivity problems,
there is no substitute for actually using the network.

DataPower offers three main diagnostic tools to help
answer questions of basic connectivity—ping, traceroute, tcp
connection test.

The idea behind these facilities is simple—to answer the
questions "Can I connect?" and "If not, why?"

Often the CLI versions of these commands are most
helpful—after all, the problem might prevent access to the
WebGUI and SSH, leaving only out-of-band or lights-out
management for performing diagnostics.

Ping

DataPower's ping command is similar to the distributed platform ping—it sends an ICMP echo request and expects an ICMP echo response back.

Ping is available on the "Troubleshooting Panel" in the WebGUI and as the "ping" command in the CLI. It has a number of uses. See Figure 1-21 and 1-22 for the CLI and WebGUI ping examples.

```
idg# ping 192.168.116.2
PING (192.168.116.2): with 56 data bytes
64 bytes from 192.168.116.2: seq=0, ttl=128, rtt=0.0 ms
64 bytes from 192.168.116.2: seq=1, ttl=128, rtt=1.0 ms
64 bytes from 192.168.116.2: seq=2, ttl=128, rtt=0.0 ms
64 bytes from 192.168.116.2: seq=3, ttl=128, rtt=1.0 ms
64 bytes from 192.168.116.2: seq=4, ttl=128, rtt=0.0 ms
64 bytes from 192.168.116.2: seq=5, ttl=128, rtt=0.0 ms
6 packets transmitted, 6 received, 0% loss, time 6012ms
idg#
```

Figure 1-21 CLI ping

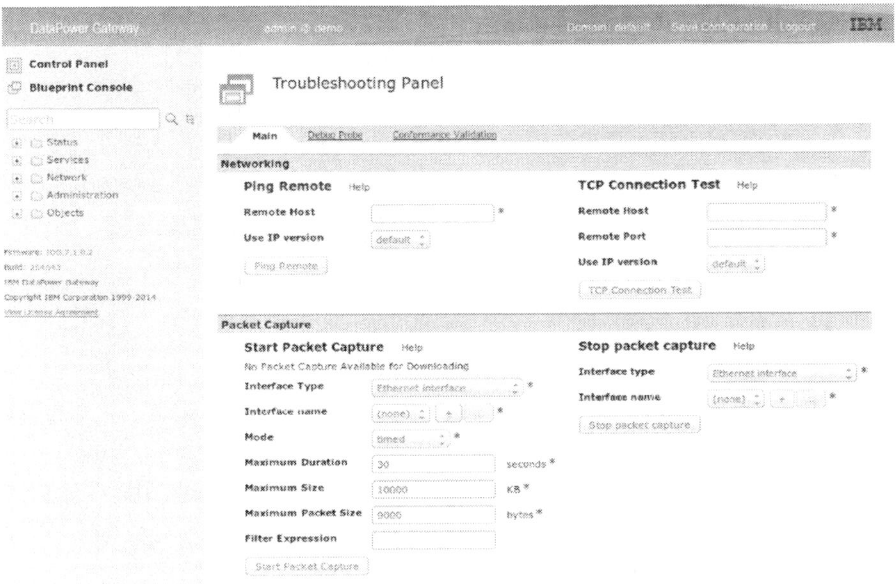

Figure 1-22 WebGUI Troubleshooting Panel

Use "ping" against any hostname or IP address. If ping succeeds, then you know both that the hostname is valid and that there is IP layer connectivity.

When ping fails, it can occur for any of several reasons. It could be that the hostname was invalid, in which case DataPower will indicate "Failed to resolve host name." It could be that there is no IP connectivity because the host is down or the address is wrong. Or it could be that there is IP connectivity, but a firewall is preventing ping specifically. Traceroute and TCP Connection Test can help disambiguate!

This is a point that bears repeating: Just because you can't ping a host does not mean that the host is not up! A TCP connection test is a more reliable test, but is inappropriate for use against routers.

Use "ping" against each next-hop router. If ping fails, likely the route is invalid.

Use "ping" against a client or a server to see if there is basic IP connectivity before digging farther into either network or service debug. Against a server, ping should also be paired with a TCP connection test. Servers listen on TCP ports, and the TCP connection test will always succeed if the appliance can connect to the service the server is offering.

Traceroute

DataPower's traceroute command is similar to the distributed platform "tracert" or "traceroute" programs. It shows each of the routers along the path by setting the IP hop count and waiting for the ICMP time exceeded message to return. It is available on the DataPower CLI as "traceroute"; it is not available on the WebGUI.

It is especially useful in identifying where something goes wrong either in routing or in a firewall since it can identify the first failing hop, whereas the other approaches only give success or failure.

Test TCP Connection

Test TCP connection is most similar to the "telnet" command when used only to see if a daemon is listening on a port— "telnet <somehost> <someport>" followed by an escape then exit. Test TCP connection succeeds only if a TCP connection can be established to the specified host and port.

Test TCP connection is available in the WebGUI on the "Troubleshooting Panel" and as the "test tcp-connection" command in the CLI.

It must be able to succeed if DataPower is to be able to open a connection to the specified host on the specified port. For instance, "test tcp-connection www.google.com 80" will succeed if DataPower can establish a TCP connection with Google on port 80 (which is http).

Note that it is likely a firewall issue if ping fails but tcp connection test succeeds. And if traceroute and ping both fail while tcp connection test succeeds, it is possible that you are traversing a network that is blocking all ICMP messages, which can be problematic.

Summary

Every DataPower developer or administrator should be aware of the concepts in this chapter.

As we look further up the stack from the network configuration, we want there to be a bright line between what is service configuration and what is network configuration. That bright line runs directly through the host alias and DNS configuration, including static hosts. Below that line is all the network interface configuration, and above it are all DataPower services.

Among the most challenging aspects of DataPower network configuration is that it is done differently for different appliances, roles, zones, and data centers. A strategy for keeping all of those differences organized is critical.

Make good use of comments on configuration objects. Develop a plan that involves all parties from the earliest possible dates. Err on the side of more host aliases than you think you need.

Verify all critical configuration. Be sure that you know the difference between configuration and status, and know how they relate to each other. Use active methods, both on the device and from remote systems to verify the validity of the network configuration of each appliance.

Finally, remember that integrating successfully, robustly, and reliably with the network is a prerequisite for DataPower to deliver value to the enterprise. DataPower integrates with the network, not the other way around. More on this in the next chapter.

Chapter 2

DataPower Advanced Networking

Introduction

In the previous chapter we presented simple DataPower network configuration and some simple configuration techniques to ensure that your DataPower services are portable from development to test to production. However, the simple, workstation-like configuration may not be appropriate for a robust datacenter production deployment. The overriding goal is to properly integrate DataPower into the target network—a goal that remains the same from the simplest development appliance to the production DMZ appliance.

What exactly do we mean by robust? How should I use all those Ethernet interfaces? What does it mean to "Integrate into the target network?"

How can I maximize availability? Tolerate the loss of any network interface? Separate network traffic? Combine it?

These are the sorts of questions this chapter hopes to help answer. These are the sorts of questions that are below the application layer, below the processing policy, and are transparent to "DataPower the proxy."

Remember, "DataPower the Proxy" cares only that clients can reach it and that it can reach servers. The things we deal with in this Advanced DataPower Networking chapter are on one hand irrelevant to DataPower "the Proxy" but are key to the success of the DataPower deployment.

The previous chapter is enough to get started on the right path. This chapter is where you will find the information required to properly integrate your appliances into each of your environments across the life-cycle of the deployment.

Conventional Wisdom Is Wrong

Of the configurable network interfaces in DataPower, Ethernet is by far the best understood.

For a long time, DataPower appliances had only four Ethernet interfaces. Conventional wisdom held that a good starting configuration involved using Ethernet interface mgt0 for management, eth0 for front-side traffic, and eth1 or eth2 for back-side traffic.

In this world, it is perfectly acceptable if all of those interfaces are on the same network and it is perfectly acceptable to have multiple default gateways and lots of host routes. In this world, the way DataPower uses Ethernet interfaces determines their purpose.

Conventional wisdom is wrong.

There is of course a kernel of truth buried in each of these premises, and there are scenarios where the classic front-side / back-side / management pattern holds reasonably true, but to identify those cases we must stop thinking about the network as something DataPower masters and start thinking about it as something DataPower must be in harmony with.

All My Interfaces / Not Just Ethernet

When the first edition of the DataPower Handbook was published, there was little need to discuss network interfaces except Ethernet. It was a CAT-5e / RJ-45 Ethernet-speaking world.

Things are different now. Now there is a great deal more to consider than just configuring IP on an Ethernet interface. We still have gigabit over RJ-45 copper, but we also have 10G Ethernet using Small Form Factor Pluggable (SFP+) transceiver modules and an array of cabling choices. In addition, we have the virtual platforms which bring its own set of networking considerations.

We had Virtual Local Area Network (VLAN) support then, but it was rarely used. Now VLANs are much more common and there are more reasons to use VLANs in DataPower.

DataPower now supports link aggregation, which allows multiple physical Ethernet interfaces to act as one logical Ethernet interface. Link aggregation is sometimes called etherchannel or NIC bonding or NIC teaming. This feature exists on layer two—the link layer. We'll discuss it in detail in this chapter.

The physical appliances have an integrated management card. It allows you to access the appliance over the network to turn the appliance on, off, and access the serial console. It is actual physical hardware based on the Integrated Platform Management Interface (IPMI) specification. It too must be considered as part of network topology and it too will be discussed in this chapter.

Yet despite all these complexities—which largely exist at the link layer and below—IP configuration remains unaffected.

When it comes to answering the question "which subnet am I on" or "Which interface should I use," it is IP routing that decides, and IP routing is the same no matter the interface type.

That is not to say that the link layer, network topology, or anything below the IP layer is not important—it is absolutely critical to a robust switching fabric. But it does say that we can treat these as entirely different subjects.

- Subject One: "How can I integrate DataPower into my link-layer network."
- Subject Two: "How can I integrate DataPower into my IP network."

From an IP perspective, it does not matter if an IP address or route is on an Ethernet interface, a VLAN interface, or a link aggregation interface. It's on an interface, and that's all that matters.

Similarly, it is of no consequence to the Ethernet, VLAN, or link aggregation interface what, if any, IP addresses or routes are associated at the link layer interface.

However, it is critically important that the link layer DataPower deployment is consistent with the link layer network infrastructure deployment. This is true no matter the technology used.

It is also critically important that the IP layer DataPower configuration is consistent with the network's IP topology. This is also true no matter the technology used.

With that in mind, let's talk a little bit about Ethernet, VLAN, and link aggregation interfaces—the directly configurable layer two network interfaces offered by DataPower. The goal here is not to configure them, but rather to understand the basic building blocks DataPower offers for robust integration into the enterprise network.

Ethernet

Ethernet is the only network interface offered by DataPower that provides the physical layer. This is true even for virtual DataPower—the appliance does not care that its Ethernet interfaces are virtualized.

There is another layer one device in DataPower—the IPMI LAN Channel. This is only present on physical appliances, and it shares the "mgt0" physical Ethernet port with DataPower's "mgt0" Ethernet interface. On those appliances, it is helpful to think of "mgt0" as a switch with three ports—the first to DataPower's "mgt0," the second to the IPMI LAN channel, and the third to the RJ45 port labeled "mgt0". This logical view is shown in Figure 1-8.

A question that comes up quite a bit is "how many interfaces should I use?" The answer to that is "Only as many as is required to fulfill business requirements and no more." We realize that it's a glib answer, but it's slightly more satisfying than "It Depends," which is the only other possible answer. So for now, resist the impulse to wire up everything.

Resist the impulse to turn every Ethernet into an aggregation. Instead, revisit this question after completing this chapter.

Remember that Ethernet interfaces are not free. Every switch port you use has a cost. It has a cost to acquire, run, and deploy. It has a cost every time excessive port usage forces the purchase and deployment of another switch that may not have been needed, then another cost for that switch's uplink and maintenance. This is among the factors to consider when answering the question "How many Ethernet interfaces should I use." How you deploy link aggregation and VLANs have a direct relationship to this cost.

There are three different ways an Ethernet interface can be used in DataPower. It can be used on its own and be given an IP layer configuration. This is the example we covered in the previous chapter.

It can be used as the basis for one or more VLANs. If used in this way, the Ethernet interface itself might or might not have an IP layer configuration, that all depends on how the IP layer integration is being done.

It can be used as part of a link aggregation. If it is used as part of a link aggregation, then it is not possible to also provide an IP configuration on the Ethernet configuration object—such configuration goes on the link aggregation configuration object instead. Similarly, if the Ethernet interface is part of a link aggregation, it is not possible to use the Ethernet interface as the basis for a VLAN. The VLAN must instead use the link aggregation.

The way each Ethernet interface should be used is dictated by the way the upstream switch port is configured.

IMPORTANT—Hierarchy of Importance

It is not the other way around! Business requirements dictate network topology. Network topology dictates switch configuration. Switch configuration dictates DataPower configuration.

The guiding principle "Integrate DataPower with the network" applies.

Link Aggregation

DataPower's link aggregation feature allows multiple Ethernet interfaces to work as a single network interface to deliver better availability and throughput.

Breaking that down, it means that if you unplug all but one of the Ethernet interfaces in an aggregation, you still have connectivity.

Link aggregation takes near-complete control of the Ethernet interfaces that are configured as members of aggregation. Link aggregation, on both the DataPower side and the network infrastructure side, is very much a part of the "Layer 2 compatibility" story. Both the appliance and the network infrastructure all the way through the DataPower Ethernet interfaces, the physical cabling, the DataPower external ports, cables, switch ports, and switch configuration must all be compatible and complimentary. This is true even if the DataPower link aggregation mode does not require the switch to be configured to perform link aggregation! We'll discuss the details later. For now, it is critical to understand that this is a holistic, broad-based layer 2 connectivity and network topology question and not a narrow "configure this port this way" sort of question.

For all of you who have requirements like "There must be no single point of failure on the network," link aggregation is how you do it.

If we are tying DataPower to the "network truck" with link aggregation, we'd have our choice of lashing materials. In this analogy, Ethernet would be mono-filament fishing line—works great, is simple, but fails spectacularly. Link aggregation would be a braided nylon rope. Also works great, is a little more complicated to make, comes in more and larger sizes, and critically does not snap at the first abrasion.

VLAN

VLANs are logical Ethernet networks. A VLAN has properties that are similar to an Ethernet network—except that there can be many VLANs on a single switch or on a single Ethernet cable or Ethernet interface. It works by adding a VLAN tag to the Ethernet frame.

VLANs are used everywhere Ethernet traffic needs to be partitioned—which is to say everywhere in an enterprise. However, much of the time the switch configuration hides the fact that everything in the switch fabric is VLAN tagged. When switches do this, the switch port is said to be in "access mode."

Switch ports in access mode look like plain-old untagged Ethernet to the device attached to the port.

But switches don't have to do that. They can be configured in "trunk mode," in which VLAN tags are exposed to the device attached to the port. This configured port will also have a "Native VLAN," which simply means that there is no tagging for that VLAN, and that the switch should interpret all untagged frames as belonging to the native VLAN.

You're probably getting the impression that VLANs can't really be used at all without the support and knowledge of the network. You are correct. But their benefit is tremendous.

What can VLANs do for DataPower?

Remember when we mentioned that you should use as few Ethernet interfaces as possible? Well, VLANs can help do that. Imagine you have five distinct networks that need to be connected. Using VLANs, you only need a single interface to integrate with those five distinct networks. With Ethernet, you'd need five.

VLANs are perfectly happy atop either Ethernet interfaces or link aggregation interfaces. But when we combine VLANs with link aggregation (which is incidentally the basis of the whole of the enterprise switching topology) we reap compounding rewards.

TIP— Link Aggregation and VLANs

Link aggregation and VLANs are the basic building blocks of enterprise switching topographies. Switches use link aggregation and VLANs among each other. Increasingly application layer devices such as DataPower and applications deployed on general-purpose operating systems are participating in these technologies. The technologies themselves are not new, but it is getting more common to see end devices making direct use of the technologies.

Consider those five distinct networks. If we wanted to connect with link aggregation and without VLANs, we would need ten Ethernet interfaces—five networks and two Ethernet interface per network to eliminate single points of failures. But with VLANs atop link aggregation, we can do the same with just two Ethernet interfaces. Figure 2-1 compares the two approaches.

Five Networks with Link Aggregation

Without VLANs in DataPower

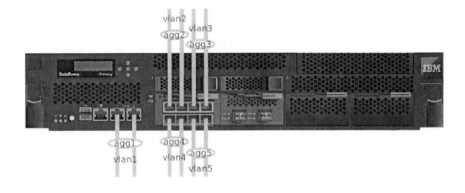

With VLANs in DataPower

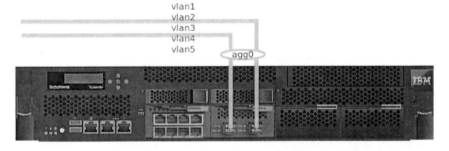

Figure 2-1 Comparison of five network integration with and without VLANs.

Not only that, but using just one aggregation gives us other advantages that we'll discuss later.

IP Network

As a discerning reader, I'm sure that you've noticed all the talk of connecting "interfaces" to "networks." We've pretty well narrowed down that an "interface" can be anything layer 2, but what about a network?

We have to admit that it's intentionally vague. Is it a subnet? Often times. Is it a broadcast domain? That's a little better. But it can also be much larger, something described by IP routing. Examples include "My trusted zone" or "Management Network" or "internetwork."

DEFINITION—Broadcast Domain

Broadcast domain: a logical computer network where each station receives broadcast MAC frames sent by any other station.

The cleanest definition is non-overlapping IP networks (for instance 10.0.0.0/8, 192.168.0.0/16) but that is not very useful—since everything that has a default route would then only be on one "network." A route just says "You get there by going this way." A default route says "You get everywhere else by going this way."

There are other considerations too. Different security zones have firewalls, and they may define what the "network" is.

After all is said and done, it is not the DataPower administrator or configuration that defines proper network integration. It is a collaborative effort that involves site networking professionals, security professionals, and data center administration.   It is then the job of the DataPower administrator to implement the resulting design.

Nevertheless, it remains the job of the DataPower administration team to ensure the appliance is integrated and maintained properly in each and every environment. And they—you—can't do that without fully participating in architecture discussions with the broader team.

First, Some Theory

Since the dawn of time (which is even earlier than January 1, 1970 at 12:00 a.m., as the UNIX people would have us believe), computers have been networked together. In fact, much like the first UNICS system (the precursor of UNIX), the first "modern network" predates the UNIX zero time point. The creation in 1969 of the ARPANET (named after the U.S. Department of Defense's Advanced Research Projects Agency) was the evolution of the first modern packet switched network, using various types of network protocols before standardizing on the ITU-T X.25 protocol over Network Control Protocol (NCP) at heady speeds of up to 50kbps.

In 1974, NCP was replaced by a more robust protocol called Transmission Control Protocol (TCP), which in 1978 was split into two separate protocols; TCP was redefined as a "higher level" protocol to provide reliable end-to-end communication, while the parts that dealt with packet routing were rolled up into a new protocol called Internet Protocol (IP). It is because of this joint heritage, where both were originally part of a single protocol, that the suite of protocols together is known as TCP/IP—the protocols with which our modern Internet and all devices connected to it communicate.

This section provides some detail about how TCP/IP works. It is framed in a context in which DataPower specific issues are presented and as a backdrop for the knowledge contained in the other chapters of the book. For a more advanced reference, we suggest readers use the TCP/IP 'bible', TCP/IP Illustrated: Volume 1: The Protocols by Richard Stevens (Boston, MA: Addison-Wesley: 1994).

Terminology

Appliances would be fundamentally useless if they could not communicate. DataPower appliances use Ethernet networking and the common networking formats and protocols of the Internet.

Figure 2-2 shows two of the network ports of an XI52 device with ten standard CAT5e RJ45 1G Ethernet ports and two 10G SFP+ slots. But what does that actually mean?

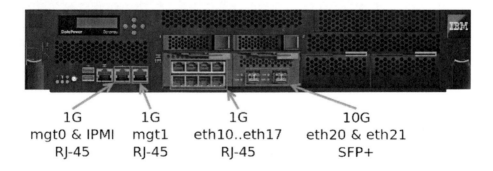

1G	1G	1G	10G
mgt0 & IPMI	mgt1	eth10..eth17	eth20 & eth21
RJ-45	RJ-45	RJ-45	SFP+

Figure 2-2 IBM DataPower Gateway Front Annotated

The devices are capable in their use of networking, and to be able to properly integrate them into your network and use them to their fullest potential, you must understand some networking technology. To explain the networking concepts, a common terminology and an explanation of the Internet are necessary.

Let's start by defining a few basic concepts. A packet is colloquially simply a block of data; it is nothing more and nothing less. In networking, a "packet" has a more specific meaning—a packet is routable. For DataPower, where our primary concern is IP over Ethernet, it is the IP layer that provides routing, so to be specific we talk about "IP packets." When we're talking the link layer in general or Ethernet specifically, the proper term is we use the term "frame."

For the IP family of protocols, the minimum routable unit—an IP packet—is called a datagram. Thus if we are talking about IP packets, we're also talking about IP datagrams. They are synonymous.

Neither packets nor frames pass judgment on what that data is; no one packet or frame is better or worse than another. Both are means to an end. For meaningful application layer communication using TCP/IP on DataPower, we let Ethernet frames carry IP datagrams which carry TCP segments which are reassembled into your application data. Examples of application data include WebGUI, SSH, front-side or back-side connections, etc.

As counter-intuitive as it sounds, don't think of an Ethernet frame as carrying your data (even though your data is wrapped up in there in some fashion). The frame is something that only exists locally, the frame can never leave the broadcast domain. The packet, the segment, and the application data however are not limited to the broadcast domain.

We'll talk more about TCP segments later. They too are an important topic, but have a different purpose and life-cycle than frames and packets.

Ethernet frames are sent between different stations on the Ethernet network. An Ethernet network simply refers to a group of stations that can communicate by sending frames to each other. A station is any device attached to the Ethernet network that might want to share information; that is, to send and receive frames. A station can be everything from computers to routers to phones to thermostats to cameras. The stations may all be similar or they might be different; there are no set rules, except that they are all stations and are connected to the same Ethernet network.

Just like we have Ethernet Frames and IP Packets, we have Ethernet Stations and IP Hosts. An IP host need not be an Ethernet Station, and an Ethernet Station need not be an IP host, but if an IP host uses Ethernet, it is both. We still use the term "station" when talking about Ethernet and "host" when talking about IP, but it's easy to get confused since commonly Ethernet stations are also IP hosts. Don't worry too much about it, just know that if someone uses the term station when talking about DataPower they are referring to something Ethernet related. Similarly know that the term host refers to something IP related.

Point-to-Point Links

Assume that there are two nodes that want to send frames to each other. The simplest form of network is a direct link between the two nodes; this is generally referred to as a point-to-point connection. This can be as simple as two computers with a null-modem cable running Point to Point Protocol (PPP) or as complicated and muddled as a Virtual Private Network (VPN). As long as the two nodes have agreed on the standards to use and the language they send, they will be able to communicate with each other. Sending data is simple; there are exactly two nodes, so when one node wants to send a frame of data, the only possible target to send it to is the other node (referred to as the "peer"). There doesn't need to be a concept of "addressing"—each node understands only "me" and "the peer."

DataPower does not offer any directly configurable Point-to-Point network connectivity options, although some are used with DataPower's infrequently used Sysplex Distributor integration option.

Broadcast Domains

Of course the directly linked network is useful in some ways, but that's not the way Ethernet works. Ethernet started as a broadcast network—connect all the stations to the same physical medium and let them communicate. An example of a shared physical medium is old-school thinnet or thicknet Ethernet. When a station wants to send a frame to one of the other stations, it puts the frame out onto the network. Because the medium is shared, all of the nodes can see all of the frames. This means that they now have to agree on a mechanism to be able to explain which station the frame is meant for; when station A wants to send data to station C, it needs to be able to say "this frame is destined for station C" so that station C knows to pick it up and use it. That mechanism is the Ethernet address.

The same principle applies in modern switched Ethernet, it's just that what was the physical medium is now a lot smarter—it pre-filters the frames it delivers to each station. And instead of "Broadcast Networks" we have "Broadcast Domains," which are just the logical version of a broadcast network where only Ethernet layer broadcast and multicast frames are guaranteed to be seen by all stations.

The idea of pre-filtering for other stations is the core difference between a switch and either a hub or shared physical medium. The switch remembers which stations (based on their Ethernet source address) it last saw on each of its switch ports. Then, when it sees a frame for a known station, it only sends that frame down the correct switch port. If it never saw destination station, or the frame is addressed to a broadcast or multicast Ethernet address, the Ethernet switch lets all the switch ports have a copy of the frame.

Routing

What if you want to talk to another station and that station is not in your broadcast domain? Simple. You can't. It's impossible. Can't be done. Might as well go home. The Ethernet frame cannot leave the broadcast domain.

Since this section does not end here, I'm sure you surmised that it's not really the end of the story. You are correct. While it is true that the frame cannot leave the broadcast domain, the IP datagram can. The datagram might have to get off the subway train, but it can transfer to a different train and continue on its journey.

In this example, the router is like the subway station. It is both an Ethernet station and an IP host, and its job is to take the IP datagrams out of Ethernet frames and put the IP datagrams back onto the correct train so the packet can continue its journey to its destination address.

If it can, the router will send the datagram in a frame to the station that is the destination host. If it can't do that, the router will instead try to send the IP packet in a frame to the station that is a router that is closer to the destination host. If it can't do that, the IP destination is unreachable, the datagram dies, and notice of its death is sent back to the sender.

In this way, an IP datagram moves from router to router. Each router takes the IP datagram out of the received frame, places the datagram into a new frame, and sends it to the next hop until at last it arrives at its destination.

Every IP host has a route table that tells the host which IP addresses are local and which must travel via a router. A router also has a route table—it is what allows the router to figure out where to send the datagram next.

In summary, this is the terminology you should understand, but you may not have drawn as firm of a distinction between station and host or between packet and datagram and frame. Hosts may be stations and stations may be hosts, but not always. All IP hosts have route tables, but only routers forward packets between networks. Routers are therefore always both stations and hosts.

OSI Layers

We've talked about "layer 2" and pounded home the frame vs packet distinction. Now let us talk about the most widely referenced network protocol layering canonicalization.

In 1982 the International Standards Organization (ISO), along with many industry players, created something called the Open Systems Interconnection (OSI) initiative. One of the outputs of this initiative was a common model for how to define layers of protocols that clearly describe interoperability between network devices and software.

The OSI model is comprised of seven layers. In this section, we discuss the first four of these, which deal with the network transports themselves; the others are application-level issues and are the subject of the rest of this volume. The layers are shown in Table 2-1.

Table 2-1□The OSI Layers

Layer	Name	Function
7	Application	Application service communication
6	Presentation	Data representation; encryption
5	Session	Inter-host communication
4	Transport	End-to-end connections; reliability
3	Network	Logical addressing; routing
2	Data Link	Physical addressing

| 1 | Physical | Physical media; signaling; binary transmission |

Nearly all DataPower function exists at the Application layer (and even then several non-OSI layers higher!). But when thinking about the network nature of the appliance, there are considerations at each layer. Also, be aware that TCP/IP does not conform to the strict OSI definitions and DataPower uses the IP family of protocols.

NOTE— Distinction Between OSI & TCP/IP Layers

The OSI layers are different than the TCP/IP layers. To make matters more confusing, there is not even general agreement about how many TCP/IP layers there are. For TCP/IP, the important layers are Application, Transport, Network, and Link, where Transport is roughly equivalent to OSI layers four through six.

The Physical Layer

In the physical layer of the OSI model, there are many standards that define exactly how data is sent. These include pin-outs, voltages, handshaking, and so on. They define, for instance, what exactly it means for the third pin on a serial connector to be +5v at a given moment. They define which wires in an Ethernet cable are used to send data, and what frequency pulses are sent at. They define when the ring signal should be sent over a 60-volt telephone wire and what frequency range wireless networks should use. Some examples of standards for the physical layer include RS-232 (serial connections), 1000BASE-TX (Gigabit Ethernet physical layer), 802.11b (Wireless Ethernet), and POTS (Plain Old Telephone System).

The physical layer may seem out of scope for a discussion on application-layer appliances—but you must remember that the appliance is still a network device, and the same kinds of issues that can affect any network device using the same technology still do apply. Indeed, the two points that follow can and do cause issues that are not easy to diagnose unless you understand how the network stack of the appliance is built!

First, consider the appliance's variety of Ethernet interfaces. DataPower offers two modes of connection: RJ-45 for its 1-Gigabit Ethernet interfaces and SFP+ PHY module slots for 10-Gigabit Ethernet. There are standards and specifications that cover every aspect of the cables and physical ports. It is those standards and specifications that govern the actual limits.

Gigabit Ethernet is specified in the 802.3ab standard (1000BASE-T) for high speeds but is also able to utilize 802.3u (100BASE-TX) for slower speeds. It is essential that the correct communication parameters are configured. This may seem trivial—doesn't this stuff happen automatically? The answer is that most of the time it does, and the appliance is, by default, configured to auto-negotiate transmission rates and duplex modes as required by 1000BASE-TX. Since DataPower only offers RJ-45 (or more correctly 8P8C) / CAT5e or better Ethernet connectivity on its 1G ports, the connectivity choices are fairly limited. This is not the case with 10-gigabit Ethernet.

TIP— Transmit/Receive Error Reasons

Seeing Ethernet transmit or receive errors on DataPower Ethernet Interfaces or on the upstream switch is a good indication of either a bad cable or a speed/duplex mismatch. There are many reasons each could occur, including using CAT5 or lower cables instead of CAT5e or better; failing or strained connectors, crimps in cables, etc. If the speed or duplex is a mismatch, check the cables themselves before attempting any manual configuration to force the speed and duplex.

DataPower's 10-gigabit Ethernet ports require SFP+ transceivers appropriate for the appliance and the upstream switch. They further require cabling appropriate for the SFP+ module. The scope of this matching problem is far too large to go into here, but most network teams have preferred patterns, gear, and suppliers that simplify this process. The authors have direct experience with 10GBASE-SR, 10GBASE-LR, and SFP+ Direct Attach Copper (DAC) cabling options for use with DataPower's 10-gigabit eth20 and eth21. This selection can only be made in conjunction with the administrator of the 10G switch to which DataPower is connected.

The physical layer has non-obvious meanings with the virtual appliances. With Virtual edition, the hypervisor owns the "real" physical layer. The DataPower guest really does not have a physical layer at all. DataPower only has the virtual one that is provided by the hypervisor's virtual switch.

Speaking of network topology, there are physical layer network topology considerations for DataPower integration into a network. Deciding which DataPower Ethernet ports should connect to which ports of which switches is a physical layer decision (with impacts farther up the stack to be sure!). It is impossible to have physical layer redundancy unless the topology supports it.

The second point has to do with the physical layer of the console interface. The serial console interface requires the parameters on both sides of the interface be the same. In the past, some DataPower appliances have been mistakenly pronounced dead and prepared for return shipment to IBM. In one case, the real culprit was a laptop reboot that had caused its serial port terminal emulation software to revert to a nonstandard setting. In another, a cable was incorrectly connected with voltages on the wrong pins making communication impossible!

TIP— Swapping Modules to Troubleshoot

Swap physical modules to troubleshoot. Get the serial or Ethernet cable working with a different device pair. Use a different switch, switch port or interface—one that is already working properly. Even getting a link from DataPower to DataPower can tell you if the DataPower port and cable are working properly! A large number of problems can be further isolated by surrounding modules under test with proven infrastructure.

The Data Link Layer

On top of the physical layer, whatever it is, lies the data link layer. This layer includes the important concept of device addressing. Physical devices on a network must be addressable in some why so that frames can be addressed to a given device. This is commonly done by agreeing on a size and format for the frame. Certain sections of the frame are given special meaning; for instance, if a standard is adopted that says that octets nine through fifteen are the destination address for the datagram, all hosts can easily see which datagrams are destined for which hosts.

The Data Link Layer is the first layer where we know something about the information being transferred. The basic unit of measurement for information on a network is an 'octet', which consists of 8 bits. Why the term octet and not byte? Because byte is platform specific, it can mean different things in different contexts. In networking, where interoperability is the goal, we use a term that always means eight bits.

Data Link Layer devices are called "stations," and they send and receive "frames." In DataPower, the data link layer is configured with the non-IP portions of the Ethernet, VLAN and link aggregation configuration objects, although link aggregation may peek into the network and transport layers depending on the scheduling algorithm.

Addressing in the data link layer refers to the MAC addresses of stations on a network. Examples of standards for the data link layer are PPP (Point-to-Point Protocol) for serial or modem connections, 802.3 (Ethernet packet format),

802.1Q (VLAN), and 802.3ad / 802.1ax for Link Aggregation Control Protocol (LACP).

Many people do not realize that, in the same way as network layer addresses can be configured dynamically at runtime, so can the physical addresses of most devices. In Chapter 1, "DataPower as a Network Device," we showed how to modify the Ethernet (MAC) address of an interface instead of using the built in MAC address. There are occasionally valid reasons to do this. One example might be when swapping out an appliance that has been physically destroyed or otherwise taken out of service; in this case, it may be prudent to configure the new replacement appliance with the MAC address of the old one so that switches and other network hardware do not consider the swap out to be a security violation, negating the requirement to flush ARP tables on every station on the network and potentially changing the switch's configuration.

If you do this, be absolutely sure that you never configure more than one interface with the same MAC address at the same time. If this happens, it can create a network outage affecting far more than just the appliances—A duplicate MAC address can disrupt the entire broadcast domain in the switching fabric!

Link aggregation is a layer one technique that allows multiple layer two network interfaces to act as a single layer two network interface in a way that is transparent to layers three and above. Link aggregation may use the same MAC address for all its links. If deployed incorrectly, link aggregation it can look like a duplicate MAC address that can disrupt the entire broadcast domain.

The Network Layer

On top of the data link layer lies the network layer. This is where devices can be given an address that is valid for more than just the broadcast domain. Of course, the address still has to uniquely identify the host in the internetwork. Addressing in the network layer is performed in a similar manner to that of the data layer—all users agree that a certain set of octets in a specific position in a packet refer to the addresses, and therefore it is obvious where a packet is meant to go. Examples of network layer standards include Internet Protocol (IP), IPv6, Address Resolution Protocol (ARP) (maps layer 2 to layer 3 for IP), Internet Control Message Protocol (ICMP), and Routing Information Protocol (RIP).

TIP— What is Meant by 'Network'?

The term"network" is sometimes used to mean "broadcast domain" and sometimes used mean "internetwork." Confusingly, we call it the network layer and it is really only needed if we are talking about an internetwork—or network of networks. This is another way of saying a network of interconnected broadcast domains and point-to-point links. The Internet is the most famous internetwork.

Much of the configuration and status discussed in Chapter 1 has to do with the network layer—IP addresses, IP routes, ping, "show netarp" are all network layer related.

The Transport Layer

Finally, on top of the network layer is the transport layer. The transport layer is responsible for providing an end-to-end connection between two hosts, regardless of where they lie on the internetwork. It may use techniques such as flow and error control, and some more reliable transport protocols will retry packets that fail in order to keep track of connection state. Common standards for transport layer protocols are Transmission Control Protocol (TCP), User Datagram Protocol (UDP), and Point-to-Point Tunneling Protocol (PPTP).

TCP is DataPower's most important protocol. All administrative connections and the vast majority of client connections will be TCP. The main exceptions are that NFS can use UDP instead of TCP, and both Syslog and SNMP use UDP.

There are transport layer configuration artifacts all around DataPower configuration. TCP Ports are configured throughout the appliance. DataPower Services listen on them. DataPower connects to them.

Since the transport layer is also responsible for segmentation, retransmission, timeout, and flow control, most latency issues are ultimately problems at the transport layer. It is therefore sometimes necessary to understand in a robust fashion the way TCP behaves in order to explain behaviors seen in DataPower—because the underlying reasons are observed due to TCP layer segmentation, retransmission, timeout, and flow control.

OSI Conclusion

We have described the four layers of the OSI model applicable to DataPower as a network device. A packet that is being sent over a network from one host to another is like a set of nesting Russian dolls, each layer providing just enough that to understand the next layer, and each layer fitting neatly in the previous layer. Different layers have different artifacts, some of the more important are the MAC address and the IP address, the TCP and UDP ports.

We did not discuss the session, presentation, or application layers in detail. The session layer is entirely embedded within the appliance configuration. Traditionally this is provided by the POSIX sockets API. DataPower offers SSL, which is a presentation layer artifact. In fact, the primary difference between HTTP and HTTPS is that HTTPS uses SSL in the session layer.

TCP/IP Primer

The goal of this chapter is not to "teach you everything you need to know" about TCP/IP and friends, but rather to give enough of the specifics about IP family to understand, explain, and troubleshoot DataPower function from the point of view of the network.

We'll get our hands dirty and look into TCP, IP (both v4 and v6) and ARP / Neighbor Discovery, but we will only scratch the surface of these topics. Careers have been made on smaller topics, and there are many good resources. For our purposes, we'll focus on the aspects of TCP/IP that most directly affect the way DataPower is deployed and debugged.

From the point of view of the DataPower professional, it is not critical to understand all of the details of how TCP/IP works, but it is very helpful to understand how TCP/IP governs the most fundamental relationship DataPower has with the outside world.

Transmission Control Protocol

TCP, or Transmission Control Protocol, is a (mostly) transport layer protocol. It's job is to take a byte stream of data from higher layers and make sure that it all gets to its connection partner. Let's unpack that a little further.

TCP is connection oriented. Like when you call home and you talk to your mother. It is just the two of you (and perhaps the NSA). No one else can interrupt, it's not a conference call. Even Dad has to wait his turn. This is the nature of a connection—it is one to one at a point in time. It's like a conversation.

We say that TCP is reliable because it ensures that everything you say to Mom she will hear, and vice versa. That is not to say the line can't be abnormally disconnected, but if that happens, you'll both know.

TCP guarantees in-order delivery. When you tell Mom that you "put on your new pants" and "went shopping," TCP guarantees she won't think you left the house in your skivvies.

None of these properties are provided by the lower levels. In a packet switched network, IP datagrams can be delivered out of order. They can be duplicated. They can be lost.

But if a TCP segment is delivered out of order, TCP puts it back in the correct order. If a TCP segment is lost, TCP understands how to resend it. If a TCP segment is duplicated, TCP knows how to ignore it.

None of this is free, of course. It takes a buffer to put packets in order. It takes a buffer to keep sent data that might need to be resent. It takes time for the TCP segment to get from one end to the other, and more time to figure out that a segment is lost, more time again to request for the resent segment to arrive, and more time again to know that the resent segment arrived safely.

Too much resending isn't good either, so TCP tries to avoid sending "too much too fast" by starting slow and gradually increasing what it sends.   This largely explains why it is generally better to use HTTP keep-alive than not—no need to start slowly for every HTTP request. Keep this in mind when configuring your DataPower service objects!

TCP Ports

A port is a 16-bit number that helps identify a TCP connection. A TCP connection is uniquely identified by the combination of the two IP addresses and two TCP ports, one from each "end." Any IP address and port combination can only be used for one thing at a time—this is true for both the client and the server.

On the server, there can only be one HTTP daemon listening on port 80 of 1.2.3.4. There can be another HTTP daemon on port 80, but it'd have to be listening on a different IP address. Or there could be another HTTP daemon on 1.2.3.4, but it'd have to be listening on a different port.

TCP clients normally use ephemeral ports when they initiate TCP connections. These ports are chosen by the operating system and are temporarily assigned to a single TCP connection. By convention, lower numbers are used for well-known services, and higher numbers are used as ephemeral ports. An ephemeral port can be reused, but TCP must first wait to ensure the close was properly received by the other side. This is the TCP state TIME_WAIT.

DataPower, as an "Application Layer Proxy," is both a client and a server. You configure some TCP ports directly—WebGUI, SSH, HTTP Service, and Front Side Protocol Handlers each require a TCP port upon which to listen.

Destination ports are also configured directly—this is the remote port in configuration objects. The simplest example is the TCP Proxy Service where a remote host and remote port are directly specified.

Ephemeral ports are different. Every TCP connection the appliance originates uses an ephemeral port. Whether it is the CLI command "copy http://myhost/firmware/fw.scrypt3 image:fw.scrypt3" or a backside connection, it uses an ephemeral port. DataPower does not allow you to control the source port for most back-end connections.

"Network Settings" has a "starting ephemeral port" value that defaults to 10000. This means that the appliance will only use those ports 10,000 and above as ephemeral ports, but it equally means that you should only use ports below 10,000 as the port for every service.

TIP— Keep TCP Ports Below the Ephemeral Range

Ensure all services use TCP ports that are below the ephemeral port range in network settings. If a service is within the ephemeral port range, restarting the service can fail unexpectedly.

TCP and Application Layer Errors

Generally speaking, application layer function is only broadly aware of TCP layer errors. DataPower is no exception. Nevertheless, there are ways to figure out if something went wrong below the application layer:

If the port is already in use on the same IP address / TCP port pair, another service cannot use the same pair. This will result in an error for the second-in service. The first service in gets to keep using the port, and the second service will see an error and will not have a LISTEN port. This sort of error can only be seen at service start or restart, and can also happen when an ephemeral port is used as the local bind port.

When a TCP connection is established, either side can send a TCP Reset. This tells the other side that no graceful close should be performed and that the connection is just plain dead. It may look like an early close, or there may be additional error information, but knowledge that it was a RST vs FIN (Reset vs connection-close) can help figure out what happened.

Many times there are additional protocols run atop TCP. These protocols describe how and when the underlying TCP connection should be closed. HTTP does this. Under such circumstances, an unexpected close (whether RST or FIN) will appear as an error in the HTTP layer whether or not it is associated with a FIN or a RST.

Lastly, TCP or the application can timeout. It happens—computers are turned off, mobile phones enter dead spots, connectivity can be lost. Under such circumstances, TCP will continue to attempt to retry for a remarkably long period of time, on the order of minutes before determining that a connection cannot be established. Once a connection is established, there is no TCP layer timeout—it is entirely the DataPower configuration that governs timeout.

DataPower timeouts are set in three main ways. Many service objects have their own front side and back side timeouts. The User Agent has the configuration for the default timeout for a processing policy, and some extension functions have an explicit timeout parameter.

INFO— More Info on DataPower Timeouts

http://www-01.ibm.com/support/docview.wss?uid=swg21469404
describes DataPower several DataPower timeouts

http://www-01.ibm.com/support/docview.wss?uid=swg21613359
describes DataPower front-side timeouts

TCP and Application Latency, Bandwidth, and Throughput

You know the Ethernet speed. You know the amount of data. What more do you need to calculate how long a transaction will take? We have all the terms required, it's just simple algebra, right? Not so fast! TCP does not work that way!

We also already talked about starting slow. That can certainly be a factor, but it's not enough, We already talked about recovering from errors. It is true, that takes time, and too much loss will cause transfers to take a very long time. But not for the reason you might think.

The reasons are all about buffers used by each side of the TCP connection. The stack only allows each TCP connection to use a certain amount of memory for the send buffer and for the receive buffer. The TCP stack on one side won't send unless it knows that the TCP stack on the other side is ready. Similarly, the TCP stack on one side has to keep everything it already sent until it receives the acknowledgment from the TCP stack on the other side that the segment was successfully received.

This is the TCP window size. Every TCP header advertises it. It represents the maximum number of unacknowledged octets that are permitted.

Because of the way TCP window works, there can be at most one window's worth of unacknowledged data at a time. Any less is fine, but any more is disallowed because it would be at best wasteful—the segment would arrive and the host would have no place to put it, so it would be discarded. This means that every round trip time (RTT) there can be at most one window's worth of data transferred, which means the TCP theoretical maximum throughput is the receive window divided by the round trip time.

TIP— Latency Clarifications

Be careful when talking about latency. When talking about TCP, it means the round trip time. But when talking about a transaction and when viewed in the DataPower log, it means something completely different. Generically, latency is the period of time between the stimulus and a reaction, so the term applies in a broad range of contexts.

The application layer—the DataPower service—will see everything that happens in TCP and below as latency. If there is enough loss and retransmit to dramatically slow the delivery or receipt of data with the other side of the TCP connection, it looks like latency to a non-streaming DataPower service.

Which brings us to one way that the DataPower developer can limit latency—use streaming. Streaming in DataPower is often not possible due to the nature of the service, but if it is available it can dramatically lower application layer latency.

Let's look at a simple case: under normal circumstances, it takes two seconds to transfer the request to DataPower, and two seconds for DataPower to transfer to the back-end, a second of back-end think time, and a negligible amount of time for the "success" response to be received by DataPower then by the client.

Without streaming, the overall transaction takes 2 + 2 + 1 = 5 seconds.

With streaming, the transfer from the client to DataPower and the transfer from DataPower to the back-end happen nearly simultaneously—DataPower does not need the entire transaction at the same time. So the overall transaction takes 2 + (the same 2, so 0 more) + 1 = 3 seconds.

Internet Protocol

IP, or Internet Protocol, is the primary OSI network-layer protocol used on the Internet and within intranets. IP provides addressing and routing so that higher-level IP family protocols like TCP and UDP can function.

IP is the protocol that lets two hosts communicate with each other. But for two applications to communicate with each other a higher-level protocol, usually TCP or UDP, is required. IP by itself does not deliver data to an application—it needs that higher-level protocol. TCP is so prevalent as that higher-level protocol that we frequently see "TCP/IP" written together as if one does not exist without the other. Of course they do, but the prevalence of the TCP/IP combination is too strong to ignore, and that also applies to DataPower.

There are two very different types of places that Internet protocol is configured on a host like DataPower. The first is its network interfaces—the Ethernet, link-aggregation, and VLAN configuration objects. The network interfaces hold the host's IP addresses and IP routes.

The other kind of place we see IP configuration is "everywhere." Every time a service is configured with a bind or listen address, it is IP configuration. Every time a back-end service is called, it uses an IP address. This is true even if the IP address is abstracted away by a DNS name, a DataPower DNS static host, or a DataPower hostname.

TIP— Abstracting Bind or Listen Addresses

Abstract out bind addresses or listen addresses with host aliases, that way you can be both specific about the bind address of a service yet let it be portable as the DataPower configuration is deployed on different appliances and in different environments.

TIP— Using DataPower DNS to Abstract Addresses

Abstract out destination addresses using DataPower DNS static-hosts or enterprise-grade DNS so targets need not change as the DataPower configuration is deployed in different environments.

Any host's IP configuration must be appropriate for the network or networks to which the host is connected, and DataPower is no exception. Addresses, subnets, and routes are configured on the host, but they are not of the host. They describe how the host interacts with the rest of the IP world and they define how the rest of the IP world interacts with the host. The host's IP configuration must satisfy the integration requirements with every internetwork the host participates in.

There is only one way to ensure that a host has a proper and valid set of IP layer interface configurations—work with the network administration and architecture team responsible for the network.

Your task in configuring networking, and especially IP layer networking in DataPower is to simultaneously satisfy the integration requirements of every internetwork connected to DataPower.

Let us repeat: Your task in configuring networking, and especially IP layer networking in DataPower is to match the target internetwork.

We'll spare a third repetition, but is the most critical point to consider when configuring the network and link layer properties of network interfaces in general and DataPower in particular. There is a long list of self-inflicted wounds resulting from failing to heed this key advice. DataPower integrates into the network topology, not the other way around.

IP Addresses

The IP address is the fundamental way IP hosts identify each other. A host often has several addresses, and one network interface can have several addresses.

Every IP address can have a network portion of its address and a host portion of its address. In IPv4, the network portion of the address is called the subnet. While the term subnet is often applied to IPv6 as well, it is more properly referred to as the network prefix (or just prefix) and host.

■ ■ ■ ■ ■ ■ ■ ■ ■ ■ ■ ■

TIP— IPv6 Address Notation

IPv6 addresses are written 16 bits groups in hexadecimal notation with each of the groups delimited by a colon. Any consecutive groups that are all 0 can be shortened to "::". Thus the IPv6 loopback address 0:0:0:0:0:0:0:1 is shortened to "::1"

■ ■ ■ ■ ■ ■ ■ ■ ■ ■ ■ ■

When we configure IP addresses on a network interface, we have to tell the interface the size of the network portion. Since all IP addresses are a fixed size—32 bits or 128 bits for IPv4 and IPv6 respectively—we simply write the address followed by a "/" and the number of bits that make up the network portion of the address. So to calculate the network address of 192.168.1.1/24, we first rewrite it as hexadecimal: 0xC0A80101 (192=0xC0, 168 = 0xA8, 1 = 0x01). Then we write the binary number consisting of the network length of 1's followed by 0's to fill the rest of the address space: 11111111111111111111111100000000b = 0xFFFFFF00, then we bitwise-and them together: 0xC0A80101 & 0xFFFFFF00 = 0xC0A80100 = 192.168.1.0.

IPv6 works the same way, except the numbers are 128 bits long. We will spare you further discussion of the mechanics of host and network calculation—resources are readily available—and suggest instead that there are a great many apps, tools, and web-based calculators. Our favorite is "sipcalc," which is a BSD-licensed open source console based calculator that supports both IPv4 and IPv6.

For network interfaces on broadcast networks (such as Ethernet, link-aggregation, or VLAN), the prefix tells the stack which addresses are local—meaning the next hop is directly to the host instead of to a router. The prefix in this way generates an implied route that is visible on the host's route table, or with the DataPower "show route" command.

IP addresses are not required for network interfaces, and there are scenarios where there is no need for an IP address to be configured on an interface, especially if that interface is being used for VLANs.

Also, one interface can have more than one IP address. Those addresses can be in the same subnet or in different subnets, but every subnet must be appropriate for the broadcast domain.

IP Routes

Routes answer the question "How do I get there from here?" In DataPower, routes are configured on network interfaces and the resulting route table can be seen with the "show route" command.

Each IP network configured on a DataPower interface causes an implied subnet route to be generated. For instance, if eth0 has IP address 10.0.0.10/24, there would be an implied subnet route for 10.0.0.0/24. If 10.0.0.11/24 were also added to eth0, there would be no new implied route—there is already a route for 10.0.0.0/24 on eth0. However, if 10.0.0.12/24 were added on eth1, then eth1 would get a local route for 10.0.0.0/24 as well. These routes are easy to identify because the next hop portion of the route is always all 0's. This principle applies to both IPv4 and IPv6.

It is the route table that determines which interface should be used to communicate with each host. When a host wants to communicate with another host, it looks in the route table, starting with the most specific routes (those with the longest network prefix). In this way, when communicating with 10.0.0.100, a route for 10.0.0.0/24 always beats a route for 0.0.0.0/0.

TIP— Default Routes/Default Gateways

A default route or a default gateway is just a route that matches every IP address. That is to say, the prefix length is 0. A default IPv4 route is a route for 0.0.0.0/0 and a default IPv6 route is a route for ::/0.

Sometimes, a host knows what its source IP address will be when it needs to communicate with another host. For instance when a client opens a TCP connection to a server, both client and server must use the same address and port pairs, only reversed. The local address and local port on DataPower must be the foreign address and foreign port on the client, and vice-verse.

Sometimes a host does not know which of its IP addresses it should use as the source IP address for a TCP connection. For instance, assume you have three interface addresses and five routes—127.0.0.1/8 (loopback), 10.0.0.10/24, 10.0.0.0/8 via 10.0.0.1, 192.168.0.10/16, and 0.0.0.0 via 192.168.0.1. Now say it wants to fetch http://10.1.2.3/. Which source address would it use?

Intuitively we say 10.0.0.10. But the stack is not intuitive. It starts with the most specific route, the one with the longest prefix. That's 10.0.0.10/24. It asks the question "Is 10.1.2.3 in 10.0.0.10/24?" We can calculate that 10.0.0.10/24 has hosts 10.0.0.0-10.0.0.255, so we know that 10.1.2.3 is not in that range.

The stack moves on to the next most specific route. "Is 10.1.2.3 in 192.168.0.10/16?" No it is not. The stack moves on. "Is 10.1.2.3 in 127.0.0.1/8 or 10.0.0.10/24?" No. The stack moves on. "Is 10.1.2.3 in 10.0.0.0/8?" Yes, so the stack knows that it should pick 10.0.0.10 as the source IP address and use 10.0.0.1 as the router to reach 10.1.2.3. It never has to inspect the final route, the default gateway.

Notice how in this example the stack worked from the most specific routes to least specific? First it did the /24, then the /16, then the /8's. It never had to look at the /0.

The same process is used when sending every datagram, although this process is somewhat modified by DataPower's default use of source based routing which we'll discuss a little bit later. Normally, hosts use destination based routing and do not consider the source address when sending a datagram.

When a host has two routes that are equivalent, which happens when there are multiple ways to reach the same network, it is indeterminate which route the stack will pick to reach that network. Again, DataPower's use of source routing help resolve the tie, but source routing does not help unless the source IP address is already known. The most common way the source address is already known is when a client connects to DataPower. When DataPower connects to another host, such as a back-end connection or side-calls, source routing does not come into play and the equivalent routes remain.

Fortunately, IP routing allows the specification of a metric, or cost, for each route. If there are multiple routes to the same destination, the route with the lower metric, or cost, is always chosen. In this way the metric can be used to favor one route over another.

TIP— Disambiguating Routes Based on Metric

Beware disambiguating routes based on metric. It is a useful technique for narrow circumstances, but the first and best approach is to not have multiple routes to the same network. Especially avoid having multiple default routes.

Special IP Addresses

Most IP addresses used with DataPower are garden-variety unicast addresses, but there are some exceptions.

All IPv4 hosts have the IPv4 loopback address, 127.0.0.1/8, and DataPower is no exception. Similarly the IPv6 loopback address is ::1/128. Expect to see these addresses in the "show ipaddress" status provider on DataPower.

TIP— 0.0.0.0 or :: as the Local IP Address

When configuring DataPower services, you may see 0.0.0.0 or :: as the local IP address. This is not an IP address that will ever appear in a datagram—it is simply a convention that indicates the service should listen on every IP address available to DataPower.

IPv4 offers three private address ranges: 10.0.0.0/8, 172.16.0.0/12, and 192.168.0.0/16. These are addresses that can be used within a home or organization but which cannot be routed in the Internet. Hence they are referred to as non-routable IP addresses. They are often used within homes or enterprises for hosts which either never access the Internet or for hosts which only access the Internet through a NAT or proxy device. RFC 1918 describes Address Allocation for Private Internets.

IPv6 offers a similar concept. The fc00::/7 address block as described in RFC 4193 offers similar capability, with the exception that IPv6 shuns NAT.

The IPv6 fe80::/10 address block is reserved for link local addresses. Every IPv6 enabled broadcast-capable network interface (such as DataPower's Ethernet, VLAN, or link-aggregation interfaces) has a link local address. The remainder of the link-local address is calculated from the MAC address of the interface.

A Virtual IP Address, or VIP, is an address that is in some way both associated with a host and not associated with a host.

It is commonly used for NAT (Network Address Translation) and load balancing—both cases where a single IP address is associated with changeable variety of hosts.

With DataPower, there are two major ways that VIPs are used, and both have to do with load balancing. If DataPower is used in conjunction with an external connection-based load balancer, then the external load balancer will have a VIP and will send some of the connections for the VIP to each of the DataPower appliances in the cluster. With an external load balancer, DataPower is not directly aware that it is part of a cluster. However, DataPower and load balancing teams still must work together to develop a topology that is satisfactory to both teams.

If DataPower's standby control or self-balancing features are used, a VIP is used for similar purposes, except the VIP is configured directly in DataPower instead of on the external load balancer. Each DataPower appliance is aware of the VIP, and each is expected to be equally capable of handling connections to the VIP. We'll talk more about standby control and self-balancing in Chapter 3, DataPower High Availability.

Multicast IP addresses are special because they allow delivery to a group of hosts instead of only to a single host. DataPower uses IP multicast only for Service Level Monitoring (SLM) and Standby Control. SLM can use routed multicast—provided your internetwork supports it. The selection of a multicast address for multicast SLM must be made in conjunction with the network administration team. Standby Control on the other hand is based on HSRP (Hot Standby

Router Protocol), and uses the special, assigned, non-routable all-routers multicast address 224.0.0.2.

There are other "special" IP addresses around—we've not talked about broadcast. We have not talked about other forms of dynamically assigned addresses, or other IPv4 and IPv6 reserved ranges. And we have only just scratched the surface of multicast. Yet what we did cover are the most critical aspects of addressing that one encounters in conjunction with DataPower.

DataPower IP Modifiers—Network Settings

The DataPower Network Settings configuration page offers a number of ways to alter the appliance's behavior at the IP layer. It is critical to keep in mind that under normal circumstances these settings should not make any difference in the behavior of the appliance. Network Settings are found in the WebGUI under Network, Interface as seen in Figure 2-3.

TIP— Investigating Non-Error Path Behavior

If any of these network settings actually change non-error path behavior, you should take a close look at the network topology, engage your network team, and be sure that what you are doing is really what you should be doing.

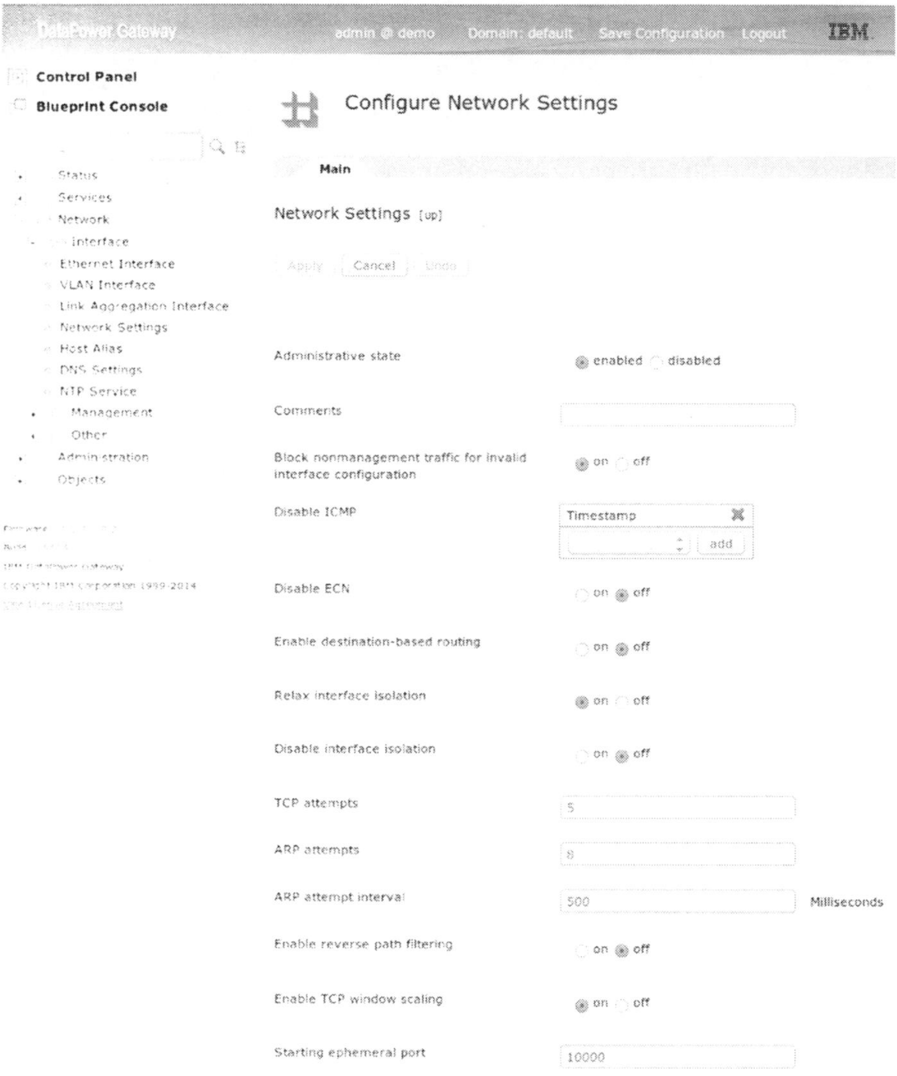

Figure 2-3 Configure Network Settings Screenshot

Destination Routing

DataPower defaults to having Destination Routing disabled. Destination routing is the "traditional" way routing is performed—only the destination address is considered. With destination routing disabled, DataPower considers both the source IP address and the destination IP address of each IP datagram in determining the next hop. This is referred to as source routing.

Source routing only gives a different answer than destination routing if: 1) The source address is already known; and 2) more than one network interface has a route that can reach the source.

Let's dive a little deeper into what each of conditions are, then look at an example where they are met and not met.

When is the source address already known? For TCP, there are two ways. If DataPower is acting as the client and initiating the connection, then DataPower chooses the source address based on the route table. If DataPower is acting as the server and a client is connecting to DataPower, then DataPower must use destination IP address from the client's connection as the IP source address.

Consider a virtual DataPower where eth0 and eth1 are both connected to the same host-only virtual network. We'll give eth0 address 192.168.1.10, and we'll use that for SSH. We'll give eth1 address 192.168.1.20, and we'll use that for other DataPower services. This topology with two NICs in the same network is shown in Figure 2-4. Note that this example could just as easily apply to mgt0/eth10 on a rack-mounted appliance.

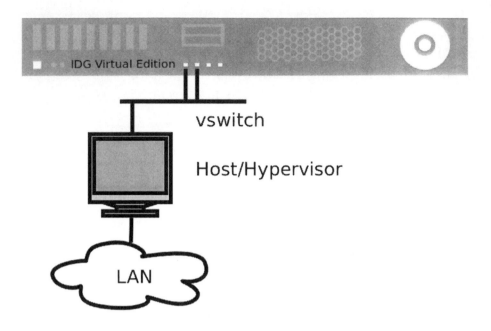

Figure 2-4 Two NICs in the same network

With this configuration, what happens when DataPower tries to ping 192.168.1.1? Will DataPower use eth0 or eth1? This is a bit of a trick question—it's not possible to know. It is indeterminate. With either source routing or destination routing, DataPower simply chooses the first route that it finds that matches (and you can't know the order). It might pick eth0 and it might pick eth1, both are equally good.

On the other hand, if 192.168.1.1 pings 192.168.1.10, and DataPower is using source routing, the response will always leave via eth1. Similarly if 192.168.1.1 pings 192.168.1.20, DataPower always sends via eth2. This is because with source routing, DataPower only considers routes on network interfaces that have the source address. Effectively DataPower uses its per-interface route table.

With destination routing, there is no per-interface route table and DataPower simply evaluates from most specific to least specific, lowest metric to highest metric. If there are ties, one will win but we can't know which.

This example also demonstrates a fundamental limitation of multiple interfaces on the same subnet—there are no circumstances that allow routing to determine when to use one interface and when to use the other. A connection to a back-end server is as likely to use the link-aggregation made up of two 10G NICs as it is to use a single 1Gbit Ethernet if both the 1Gbit Ethernet and 10Gbit link-aggregation are in the same subnet.

TIP— One Interface per Subnet

Have at most one interface in any subnet.

However, source routing can be effectively used to dedicate a specific interface to, say, device management and still avoid the problem of unintentionally using a slower interface for production data.

TIP— Message/Admin Interface Separation

Just because you can do this does not mean you should. There may be an important, specific reason why a different physical interface should be used for device management even if the network itself does not separate these functions.

How can we use source routing to ensure we use eth1 for management and eth2 for data if eth1 and eth2 are on different subnets in the same network? Consider the route table in Table 2-2

Table 2-2 Example Route Table

Destination	Interface	Next Hop	Metric
10.0.0.0/24	eth0	0.0.0.0	0
10.0.1.0/24	eth1	0.0.0.0	0
10.0.0.0/16	eth0	10.0.0.1	500
10.0.0.0/16	eth1	10.0.1.1	0
10.0.0.0/8	eth1	10.0.1.1	0

When DataPower initiates a connection (such as to a back-end server), the back-end server will never be in the management subnet (10.0.0.0/24). For every other address the appliance can reach, the address on eth1 will be chosen. If the back-end server is 10.0.2.3, which is in 10.0.0.0/16, then eth1 must be chosen because metric 0 is preferred over metric 500. If the back-end server is 10.1.2.3, which is in 10.0.0.0/8, then only eth1 has a matching route. If the back-end server is 1.2.3.4, then there is no matching route and no connection can be made.

However, if there is an incoming connection to an address on eth0, and source routing is used, then only the routes on eth0 are evaluated because only eth0 has the source address for the datagrams. This means the route table effectively looks like the per-interface example route table in Table 2-3.

Table 2-3 Example per-interface route table for eth0

Destination	Interface	Next Hop	Metric
10.0.0.0/24	eth0	0.0.0.0	0
10.0.0.0/16	eth0	10.0.0.1	500

With that effective route table, only those hosts in the 10.0.0.0/16 subnet will be able to access services bound to addresses on eth0. If a host outside that subnet managed to deliver a datagram to DataPower, when DataPower tried to respond it would discover that it has no route to that host, and the client host would time out.

Furthermore, if the WebGUI, SSH, and xml-mgmt are all bound only to an address on eth0, then source routing guarantees that all responses to clients connecting to that management address leave via eth0.

It is sometimes said that "DataPower ensures whichever interface a request arrives, the same interface is used for the response." Source routing is the feature that delivers the first half of that guarantee—the transmit half. The other half is guaranteed by interface isolation, which blocks packets that come in on the "wrong" network interface.

DataPower Interface Isolation and Reverse Path Filtering

How exactly does interface isolation know what the "right" or "wrong" interface is? That too is by IP address. Interface isolation is effectively a firewall that only allows packets in if the destination address of the IP datagram matches either a subnet configured on the network interface or an address configured on the network interface. DataPower interface isolation is controlled by the Relax interface isolation and Disable interface isolation options in Figure 2-3.

Interface isolation can be either disabled or enabled. If it is disabled, it will not block datagrams that arrive on the wrong interface, and it would be possible for someone who is both determined and has direct access to the layer 2 network to convince DataPower to respond to a packet on the "wrong" interface. Note that "wrong" is in quotes because generally the IP layer is independent of the link layer. So while one might think that an IP datagram arriving on a network interface that does not have the IP address configured won't work, in fact this is the standard way IP stacks work. Normally, IP stacks are very forgiving. If a datagram arrives on eth0 even though it "should have" arrived on eth1, the datagram is still permitted up the stack where the application will still process the data contained within.

However, with interface isolation enabled (which is the default), this cannot happen because DataPower won't allow datagrams for the wrong subnet (with relaxed interface isolation, which is also the default) or for the wrong address (with strict interface isolation).

WARNING— Interface Isolation Results

If it is possible to get a different result with interface isolation than without interface isolation, please work with your network team. This should never happen!

Reverse Path Filtering is the final IP modifier. It says "If you get a datagram and it arrives on a different interface than you would use to send a datagram back to the host, then drop the packet." Think of it as ignoring knocks on the back door—you don't expect visitors there, well-behaved visitors don't show up there, so best to just keep the door locked.

TIP— Don't Enable Reverse Path Filtering

There's usually not much reason to enable reverse path filtering given the source routing and interface isolation default values.

Never enable reverse path filtering when routing is asymmetrical! Routing is always asymmetrical for DataPower's standby control and Sysplex Distributor integration features, so never use reverse path filtering if either of those features are used.

IPMI LAN Channel

IPMI LAN Channel is interesting because it really is a separate IP stack. It is the management interface that is truly different than the others—only IPMI has dedicated hardware. Only IPMI has dedicated Ethernet (even though it shares a physical port). Only IPMI has its own MAC address. Similarly, IPMI LAN Channel has its own IP address just like any other IP host on the network. IPMI LAN Channel also has its own route (a default gateway) and this route is completely orthogonal to the routes on the DataPower appliance proper.

That is not to say that the IPMI route might not be the same as a route in DataPower proper—if both hosts (DataPower and DataPower IPMI) are connected to the same network, then it is reasonable that they would both have the same route. We also expect that all other hosts connected to the same network would also have that route, so this is simply another case of DataPower IPMI acting as just another IP host on the network.

In this way, the address of the DataPower IPMI interface does not have a special address or a special route. It simply has a normal address and possibly a normal route that is specific to IPMI. To use this address elsewhere on the same network would lead to duplicate IP address and connectivity issues for both hosts—even if both hosts are inside the same black box that is DataPower.

Often times there is a management network in the datacenter that is used for tasks such as switch administration, remote keyboard-video-mouse solutions, and integrated management modules. These kinds of services are similar to the function that IPMI LAN Channel provides. It provides a way to remotely turn the power on and off. It allows remote IP based access to the serial console. In this way it can be considered a management interface. However, it cannot be used for the WebGUI, SNMP, SSH administration, or other application layer DataPower management services.

IP Summary

IP layer configuration is the core of proper integration into a network. This is the configuration space where mistakes and misunderstandings lead to significant, hard-to-correct production issues.

From a DataPower administration perspective, the best practice is to configure DataPower networking to the site network architecture and administration teams' specifications. There is simply no need to do anything else.

From a network architecture perspective, the best practices for DataPower are similar to the best practices for any IP host. Use a single interface (no matter the type) to connect to a single network. IP routing should be clear and deterministic and testable. Keep It Simple.

Watch out for these warning signs:

- Having more than a few routes on any interfaces
- Multiple interfaces in the same subnet
- Multiple routes to the same subnet with the same prefix
- Having any host-only routes (/32 IPv4 routes or /128 IPv6 routes)—after all, it was required because "normal" routing was wrong, which means, well, that "normal" routing is wrong.

ARP / IPv6 Neighbor Discovery

Moving a little farther down the stack and we have ARP (Address Resolution Protocol) and IPv6 Neighbor Discovery. Think of these as "layer 2.5"—their job is to bridge the gap between IP at layer 3 and Ethernet at layer 2. These protocols are used on broadcast physical media (such as Ethernet, link aggregation, and VLAN) to figure out the MAC address of the next hop.

Let's break that down a little. Say you're any host, or even DataPower. You've just booted and you have an IP Datagram that you want to send, and you have a route table. How do you do it?

Well, you first consult the route table. There are three possibilities: No, Local, or Via.

If the route table says "no," if it says that you can't get there from here, there is nothing else to do.

The route table might say that the address is local. If so, you'll also know the interface. But then what? This is an IP layer answer, and the Ethernet frame must be constructed with an Ethernet / MAC address. For this you will use ARP for IPv4 or IPv6 Neighbor Discovery with the destination IP address as the next hop address.

Similarly, the route table might say that the address is via a router at an address on an interface. But the problem remains—how to fill the Ethernet frame? For this you will also use ARP for IPv4 or IPv6 Neighbor Discovery, except you won't use it on the destination IP address, you'll use it on the via address, which is to say the router's IP address. You perform ARP or IPv6 Neighbor Discovery on the next hop address.

The overall mechanics of ARP and IPv6 Neighbor Discovery are similar. Both send a frame that can be seen by every station that might have the next-hop address. For ARP, this is an Ethernet broadcast—seen by every station. For IPv6 ND, this is the solicited-node multicast IP address which results in a multicast Ethernet address. Both methods result in a request that is seen by every station that might have the IP address.

In both protocols, the station that sees a request for an address it owns responds directly to the requesting station. In both cases the response includes the MAC address of the next hop.

Also in both protocols, responses are required to be cached for future repeat use, although the cache expiration policy is different.

So, back to the question of "what would you do if you were the host?" Let's say that the datagram you need to send is addressed to 1.2.3.4 and has to go via 10.0.0.1 on eth10. You would send an ARP who-has 10.0.0.1 out eth10, and when the response comes back "10.0.0.1 is aa:bb:cc:dd:ee:ff", you would remember that value then send your IP datagram addressed to 1.2.3.4 but in the Ethernet header you'd put the destination MAC address of the router, namely aa:bb:cc:dd:ee:ff.

And since you cached the request, when you have to send further datagrams through 10.0.0.1, you have no need to perform the ARP or ND because the answer is already cached.

The protocols standards define how that cache must be managed, what the expiration policy is, how they can be updated, etc. And the ARP and IPv6 ND differ significantly in this area. Specifically, ARP cache management is an important to understand for DataPower's standby control feature, which we'll discuss in depth later.

Using DataPower's IP and Link Layer Connectivity

In the context of the function of the TCP/IP stack, the underlying link layer technology is irrelevant—it simply does not matter. All of DataPower's link-layer technologies— Ethernet, VLAN, and link aggregation—offer identical TCP/IP functional properties. These are the layer 2 network technologies which provide the foundation for IP.

So if they all have the same function, what's the point? It turns out that they differentiate themselves in other ways: Availability, cost, throughput, and flexibility for starters.

First, for all these technologies it is Ethernet that is the foundation. Link aggregation bundles several different Ethernet interfaces into a single logical link—one that continues to work even if one of the physical interfaces loses link. A VLAN on the other hand takes a single logical interface and causes it to act as many logical interfaces.

Each of these are true layer 2 connectivity options. Each offers its own broadcast domain. Ethernet and link aggregation use identical frame formats, VLAN has an additional tag but it does not count against the Maximum Transmit Unit, or MTU.

In the previous chapter we already discussed how to configure a simple Ethernet interface. It turns out that it's not much harder to configure a link aggregation or a VLAN—it's just that they each relate to other network interfaces.

Remember, from an IP perspective and above, an Ethernet interface, a VLAN interface, and a link aggregation interface are all configured in the same way. Each requires proper coordination with the target network—both from an IP configuration and from a layer 2 configuration point of view.

Here we'll briefly cover the mechanics of how link aggregation and VLAN are configured. We have to start somewhere, and this is as good a place as any. If you are already familiar with network design and the purpose of link aggregation and VLANs, this is a great way to jump right into the configuration steps in DataPower. If you're not as familiar, don't worry, some sample topologies are coming up too.

Common for all link types

Most of the Ethernet configuration we discussed in Chapter 1 is actually IP configuration. Things like IP addressing, IP routing, DHCP, SLAAC on the main configuration panel and advanced settings IPv6 DAD attempts and IPv6 Neighbor discovery delay. Figure 1-2 shows the Main configuration panel and Figure 2-5 shows the advanced. These are present on every DataPower network interface type because all are part of the IP layer and it is the role of each kind of DataPower network interface to provide IP layer connectivity for DataPower services.

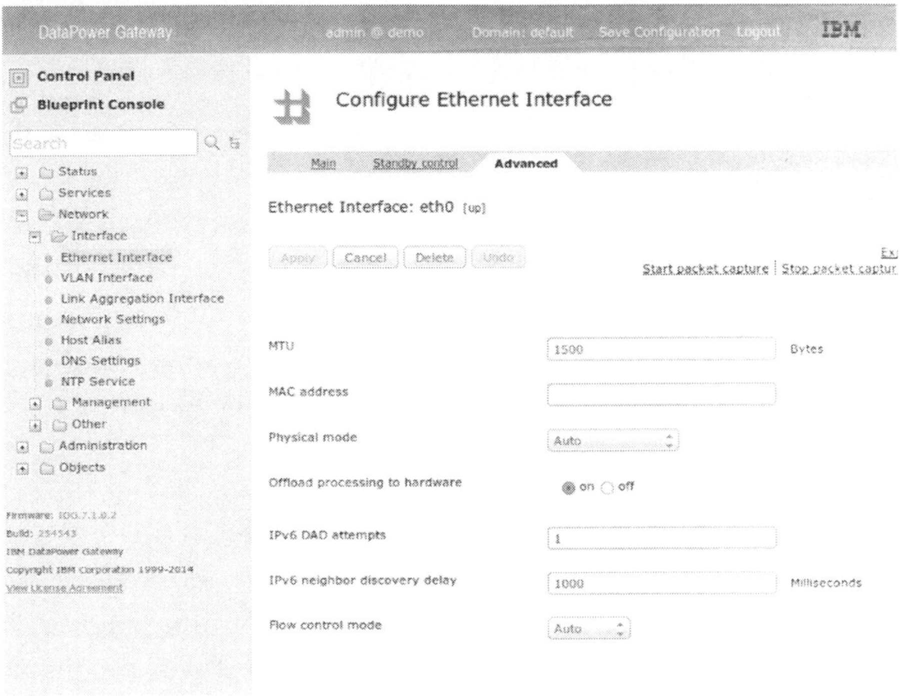

Figure 2-5 Advanced Ethernet configuration panel for discussing IP configuration

The MTU is also present on every kind of interface, but it is truly a layer 2 configuration property.

The previous chapter described how to verify and troubleshoot network configuration in general. All of that applies equally to every type of DataPower network interface.

Ethernet

Many DataPower administrators are most comfortable dealing with Ethernet interfaces. You configure your IP address and routes on an Ethernet interface as we described in Chapter One and you don't think about it too much more.

But they can do so much more. In fact, an Ethernet interface can be a useful thing even without any IP configuration at all! The other two layer 2 network interfaces DataPower offers—link aggregation and VLAN—are built atop the venerable Ethernet interface.

Ethernet interfaces can be used in three distinct ways. They can be "normal" interfaces, with an IP configuration. They can be used to host one or more VLANs, either with or without an IP configuration of their own. Or they can be used in a link aggregation, in which case that is all they can do.

Even when the Ethernet interface has no IP configuration of its own, there are still link layer properties available to configure in the DataPower WebGUI.

When "Enable for link aggregation" is on, two things happen: first, all the IP layer configuration properties become unavailable. They are in fact hidden in the WebGUI as we can see in Figure 2-6.

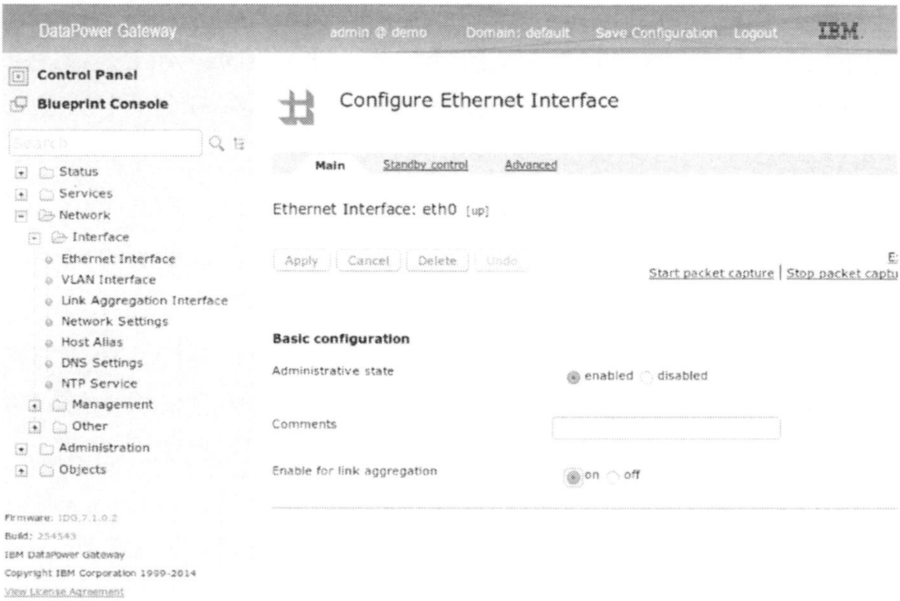

Figure 2-6 Configure Ethernet Interface with Enable for link aggregation on

Additionally, no Standby Control configuration is possible. The tab is still present but there is nothing available to configure in the tab.

On the Advanced tab, only the link layer properties remain. As you can see in Figure 2-7, only MTU, MAC address, physical mode, offload settings and flow control remain.

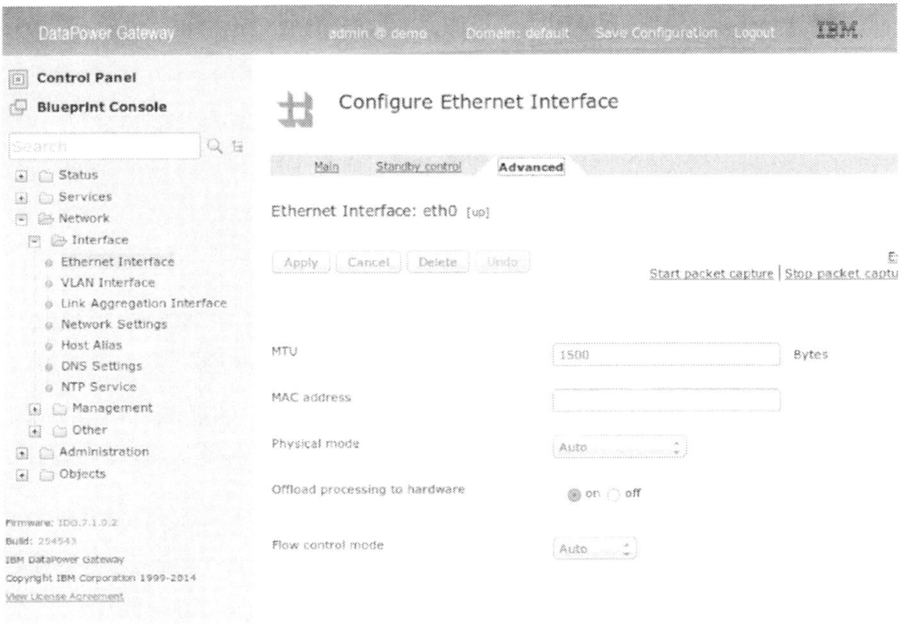

Figure 2-7 Configure Ethernet Interface with Enable for Link Aggregation on Advanced tab

The purpose of the "Enable for link aggregation" setting is to configure the Ethernet interface in a way that it is possible to use it in a DataPower link aggregation. This is the first step of deploying link aggregation.

The other settings exist in order to match the target network.

When the MTU is changed it is usually to something larger (like 9000) when the network supports jumbo frames. It is also sometimes set smaller when there is a constriction in the network and TCP path MTU discovery cannot be used, but this is a very unusual situation and it often indicates some sort of problem in the network that should be resolved.

The physical mode should generally be left at Auto. Ethernet standards for 1G and faster Ethernet require a clock sync, which effectively requires auto negotiation anyway. Yet there are still some rare situations where manual specification of the mode may be helpful—especially when connecting to switches slower than 1Gbps.

These days there are many forms of hardware offload provided by Ethernet NICs. These are generally very helpful technologies, but there are reasons one might want to temporarily or permanently disable Ethernet hardware offload.

Hardware offload can make it more difficult to understand what is actually happening in packet captures taken on the appliance. When the packet passes by the point where it is captured, it is not in its final form. It may look like an impossibly large packet. Its checksums may not be correct. Various forms of offload alter all these things, and it can be helpful sometimes to disable hardware offload for the purposes of problem determination.

It is also possible, though very rare, that hardware offload may contribute to an actual problem.

TIP— Packet Capture at Different Points

With packet capture, it is rarely possible to truly see what is in the packet. It is only possible to see what the data structure representing the packet contains when the packet passes the instrumentation point in the stack. Because of this, it is sometimes necessary to perform packet captures at different points in the network. Perhaps at the client, at the server, and at different points in between where important transformations (such as NAT) take place. Packet capture is more like detailed tracing at an inspection point than an omniscient all-seeing observer and provider of universal truth.

For both of these reasons, DataPower offers two ways to disable hardware offload. The first is to set offload processing to off as seen in the Ethernet Advanced configuration tab in Figure 2-7. The other possibility is to temporarily disable hardware offload using the action present in the links at the top of every Ethernet configuration page such as those shown in Figure 1-2 and Figure 2-5. Remember though that it is not possible to disable all offload, so don't be surprised if you still see artifacts of offload when inspecting packet captures taken on DataPower.

Link Aggregation

Link aggregation uses multiple Ethernet interfaces to construct a single aggregated interface. It is a layer 1 and layer 2 technology used to increase availability and/or bandwidth for a logical link.

TIP— Link Aggregation By Any Other Names

Link aggregation is often called NIC bonding, NIC teaming, NIC trunking, or etherchannel. Don't confuse it with "trunk mode," which describes a switch port that passes VLAN tags.

Let's break that down a bit more. Layer one—that's physical. Link aggregation uses multiple wires or fibers and treats them as one.

When DataPower is running as a guest on a hypervisor, DataPower does not generally have access to layer one. There is no "wire," there is only a vswitch. While a vswitch may be a switch too, there is no actual wire distinct from the vswitch that can fail. Because of this, link aggregation in the DataPower guest is generally not applicable. But the hypervisor may well provide link aggregation, thus giving the DataPower guest the benefits in terms of throughput and availability provided by link aggregation, the technology.

TIP— Link Aggregation Practice

You can still practice using link aggregation in DataPower on a hypervisor or developer edition—it's best to do so on an isolated vswitch such as a host-only network.

This link aggregation interface can have an IP configuration—one configures addresses, routes, standby control, and everything IP layer and above on the link aggregation interface in the same way that one would configure them on an Ethernet interface or a VLAN interface. But like an Ethernet interface, a link aggregation interface does not need an IP configuration in order to be useful—it could be used solely as the parent of VLANs.

While from the IP layer up a link aggregation interface is identical to an Ethernet interface, from the link layer down it's quite different. It is configured to take control of the Ethernet interfaces on the stack. It is configured to combine them in various ways. It is configured with different strategies of how the different Ethernet links should be shared.

The steps to configure a link aggregation are:

1. Validate the switch configuration and topology with the network team responsible for the switches you are connecting to.

2. Perform physical deployment. Ensure the proper DataPower Ethernet ports are connected to the proper switch ports.

3. On each DataPower Ethernet interface in the aggregation, enable it for link aggregation. See Figure 2-6. Set advanced settings as required in Figure 2-5.

4. Navigate to Network→Interface→Link Aggregation Interface. Add a new Link Aggregation Interface as shown in Figure 2-8.

5. Choose the correct Link Aggregation settings as agreed to in the first step. These include the proper link aggregation mode and mode specific settings.

6. Configure IP networking as shown in Figure 2-8.

7. Click Apply.

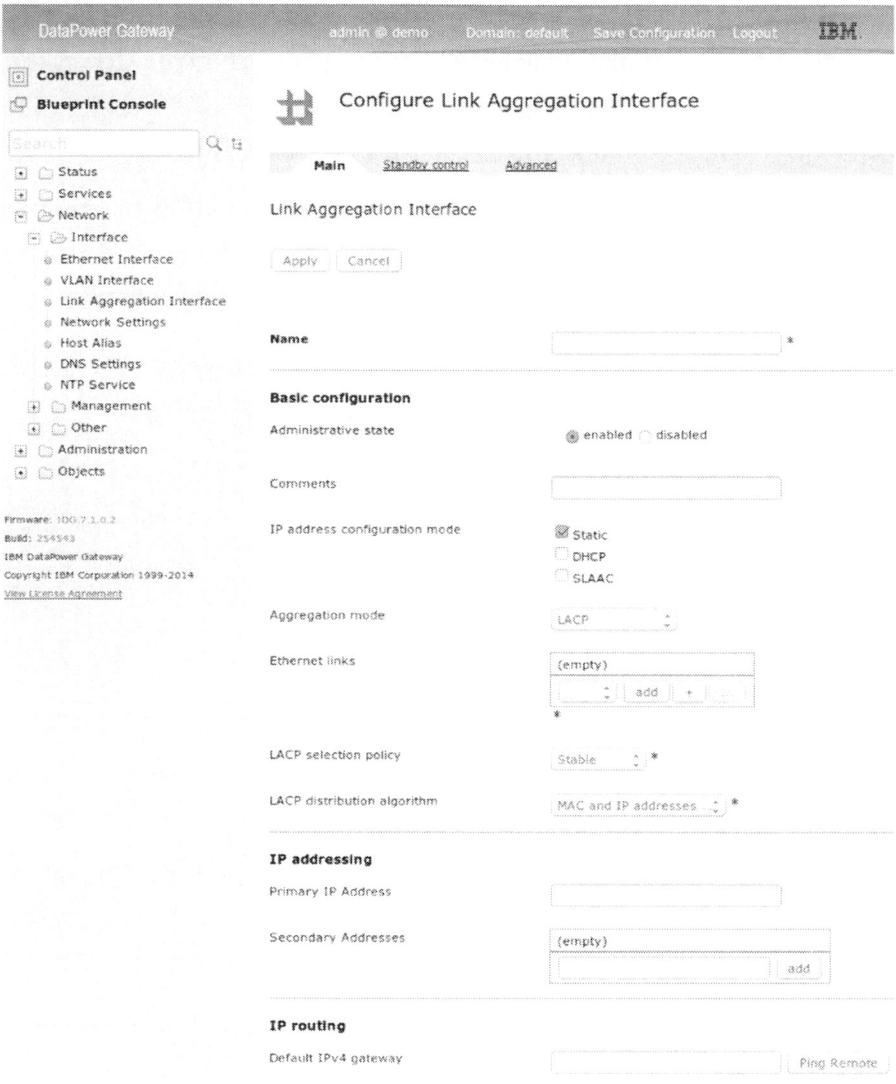

Figure 2-8 Link Aggregation Main tab with LACP aggregation mode.

There are a few important things to remember. For an Ethernet interface to be part of a link aggregation, two conditions must be satisfied. First, it must be configured so that it is enabled for link aggregation. We covered that in the previous steps. It also must not be a member of any other link aggregation.

Additionally, when an Ethernet interface is actually a link in a link aggregation, there can be no configuration changes made to the Ethernet interface. It is locked—no changes at all are possible. It loses its own identity and is only a member of the collective link aggregation.

Every link aggregation should have two or more Ethernet links. These are the Ethernet interfaces that are used together to build the aggregation. If link aggregation is a rope, then the Ethernet interfaces are the strands that make up the rope.

Aggregation mode describes how the links are combined. To keep with our rope analogy, this might be the weave. Twisted or braided? We have active-backup, transmit-based and LACP, or Link Aggregation Control Protocol.

LACP is the industry standard aggregation technology. It is widely supported by switch vendors. It is well-understood by networking professionals. Only LACP can increase both the transmit and receive bandwidth. Only LACP is a standards-defined way of performing link aggregation. Because of this, it is generally the first choice when link aggregation is needed. With LACP, the appliance and the switch communicate with each other so that each side knows which links are part of which aggregation. If choosing in a vacuum, choose LACP. But remember the first step: Validate the topology with the network owner.

Active-backup works just the way it sounds. While there are multiple links in the aggregation, only one is used at a time. But if that one link were to fail, or the switch connected to that one link fails the appliance does not lose connectivity. Active-backup only helps with availability, not with bandwidth. But it turns out that this is probably not much of an issue, especially with 10G NICs.

Transmit-based is like active-backup except that the appliance will send with all available links. This can be useful in a few narrow scenarios where the appliance needs more outbound bandwidth than inbound and LACP is not possible.

TIP— Link Aggregation Bandwidth

Remember that among the goals for link aggregation is to be able to transparently lose a single link in the aggregation and not suffer a greater loss (such as the appliance from the cluster). This means that there must be sufficient bandwidth in the link aggregation to handle the loss of one link without causing the appliance to be unable to fulfill its role in the cluster.

Each mode is useful for different circumstances. We suggest the following order of precedence in selecting an algorithm:

1. Choose the mode recommended by the network team responsible for your network.

2. Determine if link aggregation is required. If it's not part of the standard pattern used for hosts that are critical infrastructure, or this appliance will be used in a way that does not require a layer one / layer two availability strategy, then just use plain-old Ethernet.

3. If platform is virtual, don't use DataPower link aggregation. Instead use an availability strategy appropriate for your hypervisor.

4. If LACP is possible, use LACP. LACP is 802.3ad/802.1ax and is the industry standard way of doing link aggregation. Standard is good. It's also the most functional, and the only mode that offers increased full-duplex bandwidth.

5. Use active-backup. It is generally favored over transmit-based, unless a few very specific criteria are met.

6. If IO bound only on transmission, such as using self-balancing and/or the appliance workload is small requests and large responses, and LACP is not possible, and it is not possible to use a more capable network interface, then use transmit-based.

LACP offers more configurable parameters than either active-backup or transmit-based.

LACP Distribution Algorithm

LACP distribution algorithm allows configuration of the hash policy that the appliance uses to determine which frames are sent via which links. There are three options:

- Hash only based on the MAC addresses
- Hash on the MAC and IP addresses (default)

- Hash IP addresses and TCP/UDP ports.

The best option is to configure DataPower to use a strategy which is similar to the strategy used by the switch. The switch may offer multiple modes—in that case you have to know something about the nature of your traffic in order to discuss the options with the network team.

Consider the example of hashing on the MAC address. That means that every time DataPower sends an Ethernet frame to the router, DataPower will use the same Ethernet interface, possibly eth10. If the switch is using a similar algorithm, then every frame from the router will use the same Ethernet interface—but not necessarily the same one DataPower would have used. So let's say it uses eth11. This is true no matter what IP address or TCP port the packet is addressed to. Thus in this scenario, if most of the hosts DataPower is communicating with are via that one router, then the effective bandwidth to all hosts is limited by the hash to a single NIC. The source and destination Ethernet addresses are all the same, so each frame hashes to the same NIC, so the overall aggregation transmit throughput will be limited to the bandwidth available on eth10.

For similar reasons, hashing based on the IP addresses result in the throughput between IP addresses being limited to the speed of a single NIC. And it follows that hashing that includes TCP has a ceiling throughput for a single TCP connection that is the speed of a single NIC.

No matter the hashing policy, no matter if LACP is used or another mode, there is always a certain amount of unevenness in the distribution of frames among NICs in an aggregation. It can be no other way—in order to avoid out of order frames, link aggregation has to ensure that a single TCP connection always flows through the same member NIC. This is the source of the necessary uneven distribution.

LACP Selection Policy

In order to understand what the LACP selection policy does, it's first necessary to understand the concept of a LACP aggregator. And before we dig into that, let's know that there are a number of scenarios where the LACP selection policy simply does not matter.

An aggregator is a group of ports that are all configured to work together in an aggregation. When you configure DataPower to use eth10 and eth11 in a LACP aggregation, eth10 and eth11 are the same aggregator. If you then add eth12 and eth13 to a different aggregation, eth12 and eth13 are the same aggregator as each other but are a different aggregator than eth10 and eth11.

It is the same on a switch.

Now, it is possible for a single DataPower aggregation to see more than one aggregator, as might be done in building a DataPower topology that is resilient to a failure of a single switch. In this case, eth10 and eth11 might go to switch 1, and eth12 and eth13 might go to switch 2. DataPower would see two different aggregators—an aggregator for switch 1 and an aggregator for switch 2. An example of DataPower connected to two switches that are also different aggregators is shown in Figure 2-9.

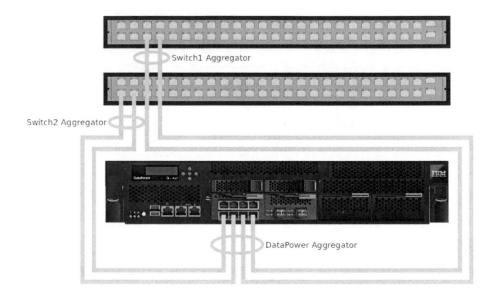

Figure 2-9 LACP with multiple aggregators

The LACP selection policy governs how DataPower chooses among multiple aggregators.

Now, we mentioned that it may not matter. This is often true—when there is only one aggregator, the aggregator selection policy has no choice to make.

There should only be one aggregator if the switching fabric uses VLAG, or Virtual Link Aggregation, which allows multiple switches to act as a single switch for the purposes of link aggregation. It is also true that the appliance will only see one aggregator if the appliance is only connected to a single switch.

Conversely, if you expect the appliance to be configured to a single aggregator, either due to VLAG or due to a single switch and it sees multiple aggregators, that is a sign of misconfiguration or of a cabling mismatch. Figure 2-10 shows a similar topology to Figure 2-9 except VLAG has been added turn the physical switches into a single logical switch.

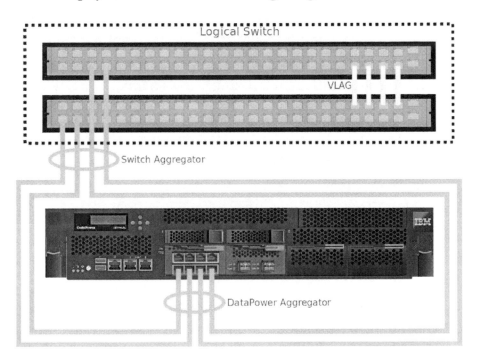

Figure 2-10 Two switches form a single logical switch with VLAG

If VLAG is not deployed and it is a business requirement to deploy redundant switches to DataPower, multiple switches are required. And if a LACP aggregation is associated with multiple switches, there will be multiple aggregators. When there are multiple aggregators, it is important to pay attention to the LACP selection policy.

The LACP selection policy offers three choices—stable, count, and bandwidth. The stable policy only changes to a different aggregator when the current aggregator has no members—it stays with the current aggregator until the bitter end. It is stable because topology changes are minimized. The count policy changes to a different aggregator when the other aggregator has more links than the current aggregator. The bandwidth policy changes to a different aggregator when the sum of the speed of the other aggregator's links exceeds the sum of the speed of the current aggregator's links. The default is stable.

Under most enterprise deployment cases, count and bandwidth result in similar behavior—the loss of one link in the active aggregator results in switching to the other aggregator. The act of switching is functionally transparent to the DataPower Gateway and to all the hosts DataPower is communicating with, but it is not transparent to the switching fabric.

The switching fabric has to respond to the MAC address of the link aggregation moving from one place in the network to another. That response, caused by spanning tree re-converging, can take from six to sixty seconds. This re-convergence time has to be considered as a factor in choosing a LACP selection policy, and also explains why stable may well be the best choice for those not terribly bandwidth constrained.

Note that VLAG does not have this issue since the aggregator does not change. If deciding in a vacuum, VLAG is better than multiple aggregators as an availability technology.

Fundamentally, DataPower has to be configured to properly integrate into the network and the architecture that is already there. It is true VLAG offers better failover, but the best strategy is the one that is proven in your datacenter with your switches and with your network team. This is the way to deliver availability for your appliance.

Link Aggregation Member Status

The Link Aggregation Member Status shows which link aggregation interfaces are associated with which Ethernet interfaces. When the link aggregation is LACP, it also shows the aggregator ID of each Ethernet interface.

As you can see in Figure 2-11, a number of Ethernet interfaces have the same Aggregator ID. When Ethernet interfaces in the same aggregation have the same Aggregator ID, they can be used together in a LACP link aggregation.

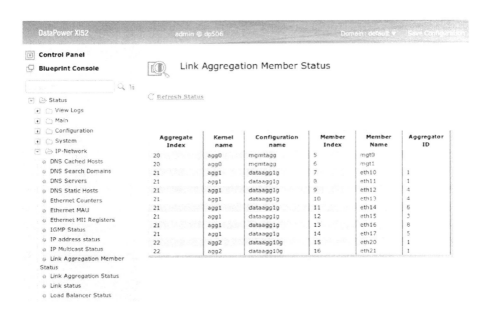

Figure 2-11 Link Aggregation Member Status Screenshot

If there is no link on an Ethernet interface and that interface is part of a LACP link aggregation, expect that the

Aggregator ID will be unique. This is the case with eth14, eth15, eth16, and eth17 in Figure 2-11.

When an Ethernet interface is in a non-LACP link aggregation, the aggregator ID will be blank. In Figure 2-11 mgt0 and mgt1 are in an active-backup aggregation so they do not have an Aggregator ID.

The Link Aggregation Member Status also shows the complete association of the low-level network interfaces with the configuration names for the aggregation and the network interfaces. You can see that the aggregation named mgmtagg contains Ethernet interfaces mgt0 and mgt1, that dataagg1g contains eth10 through eth17, and that dataagg10g contains eth20 and eth21.

Keep in mind that this is a contrived example meant to demonstrate link aggregation. Normally a single link aggregation is sufficient.

Link Aggregation Status

The link aggregation status provider shows how the link aggregation itself is operating. In the case of active-backup or transmit-based, it shows which aggregated Ethernet interface is currently active. When the aggregation is LACP, it shows all the details necessary to understand why the aggregation chose the aggregator that it chose.

The active interface field (see Figure 2-12) is only used for active-backup and transmit-based. You can see it shows which Ethernet interface is, well, active. But active has somewhat different meanings for the two modes. With active-backup, the active interface performs all sending and receiving of frames.

With transmit-based, the active interface performs all receiving and its share of the sending.

There's quite a bit more to the way LACP works. Some of the fields, like LACP hash policy and LACP selection policy should be just as configured. Similarly, the LACPDU rate is a protocol configuration property.

The Actor key and Partner key are LACP protocol artifacts and could be helpful in deep debugging of the LACP protocol, but are not normally very interesting for a DataPower administrator.

The Aggregator ID is perhaps the most important of the LACP status fields—it is what allows you to know which aggregator and thus which Ethernet interfaces are actually being used by the aggregation. Compare Figures 2-12 and 2-11. For the same LACP link aggregation interface, the aggregator ID from link aggregation status correlates to the aggregator ID in 2-11. Remember, a single LACP aggregation can be associated with multiple aggregators, or switches. The aggregator ID is the key that allows the link aggregation status and link aggregation member status to be related to each other. It is the combination of the aggregator ID, link aggregation status, and link aggregation member status that allows you to know which NICs are currently being used to transmit data in a link aggregation.

In Figure 2-12, note how for agg0, which is mgmtagg, mgt0 is active and there are two ports in the aggregation. This is consistent with Figure 2-11, where we can see that mgmtagg has mgt0 and mgt1 as members.

Also in Figure 2-12, see that agg1, which is dataagg1g, is currently using Aggregator ID four. What exactly is aggregator ID 4? We can see in Figure 2-11 that eth12 and eth13 have Aggregator ID 4, so we know that DataPower is using eth12 and eth13 for all sending and receiving associated with dataagg1g.

Comparing Figures 2-12 and 2-11 again, notice that there are only 2 ports in shown in dataagg1g. How can that be—we know that eth10 through eth17 are all configured to be in that aggregation! The answer is straightforward—this column is LACP specific and does not refer to the number of ports in the aggregation, it refers to the number of ports to the active aggregator.

The aggregator ID when the DataPower NIC does not have a link or is not connected to a switch port that is not configured for LACP is unique. It looks like it's connected to its own private aggregator.

Link Aggregation Status

Refresh Status   Help

Index	Kernel name	Configuration name	MTU	Mode	Status	Primary interface	Active interface	LACP hash policy	LACPDU rate	LACP selection policy	Aggregator ID	Number of ports	Actor key	Partner key	Partner MAC Address	MII Status
20	agg0	mgmtagg	1,500	Active-backup	OK	None	mgt0									OK
21	agg1	dataagg1g	1,500	LACP	OK			layer2	fast	stable	4	2	17	10	6c:ae:8b:e9:aa:00	OK
22	agg2	dataagg18g	1,500	LACP	OK			layer2	fast	stable	1	2	33	9	74:99:75:08:79:00	OK

Figure 2-12 Link Aggregation Status Screenshot

VLAN

A Virtual Local Area Network, or VLAN, allows a single layer 2 network interface to act as multiple layer 2 network interfaces.

VLANs are defined by the 802.1Q specification and work by adding a tag to the Ethernet frame that identifies the VLAN.

Every frame in an enterprise switching fabric is in a VLAN whether the host is aware of the VLAN or not. Subnets are associated with VLANs. Switches often hide the fact that there is a VLAN by using "access mode" on host-facing switch ports. Switch ports in access mode look to the host as though there is no VLAN present—just plain-old untagged Ethernet.

Switches can also be configured to allow certain VLANs to be trunked onto a switch port. When a switch does this, it simply allows the Ethernet frames with the VLAN tags to pass unaltered onto the switch port. Ports configured in this way are called trunked, and a trunked switch can also pass untagged frames, and this is called the "native VLAN."

DataPower VLAN interfaces have to be configured for each trunked VLAN. Conversely, if a switch port is in "access mode" or if we're talking about the "native VLAN," then DataPower's link aggregation or Ethernet interfaces are appropriate. Only use DataPower's VLAN interface when the VLAN tags are visible to the appliance.

In order to configure a VLAN, you'll need to:

- Know which VLAN IDs are trunked
- Know which network interface (Ethernet or link aggregation) hosts the VLAN
- Know the IP layer configuration appropriate for the VLAN
- Have already configured the parent Ethernet or link aggregation

At that point, the configuration process is straightforward:

1. Navigate to Network→Interface→VLAN Interface in the WebGUI.

2. Press Add to add a new VLAN Interface.

3. Name the VLAN interface something meaningful, possibly matching the naming convention from the network team.

4. Select the network type for the parent interface. The VLAN will be hosted on either an Ethernet interface or a link aggregation interface.

5. Configure the VLAN Identifier.

6. Add the IP layer configurations.

7. Click Apply.

As you can see in Figure 2-13, the only link layer configuration parameters are the VLAN ID, the outbound priority, and the fields that allow the selection of the Ethernet or link aggregation interface that the VLAN is deployed upon.

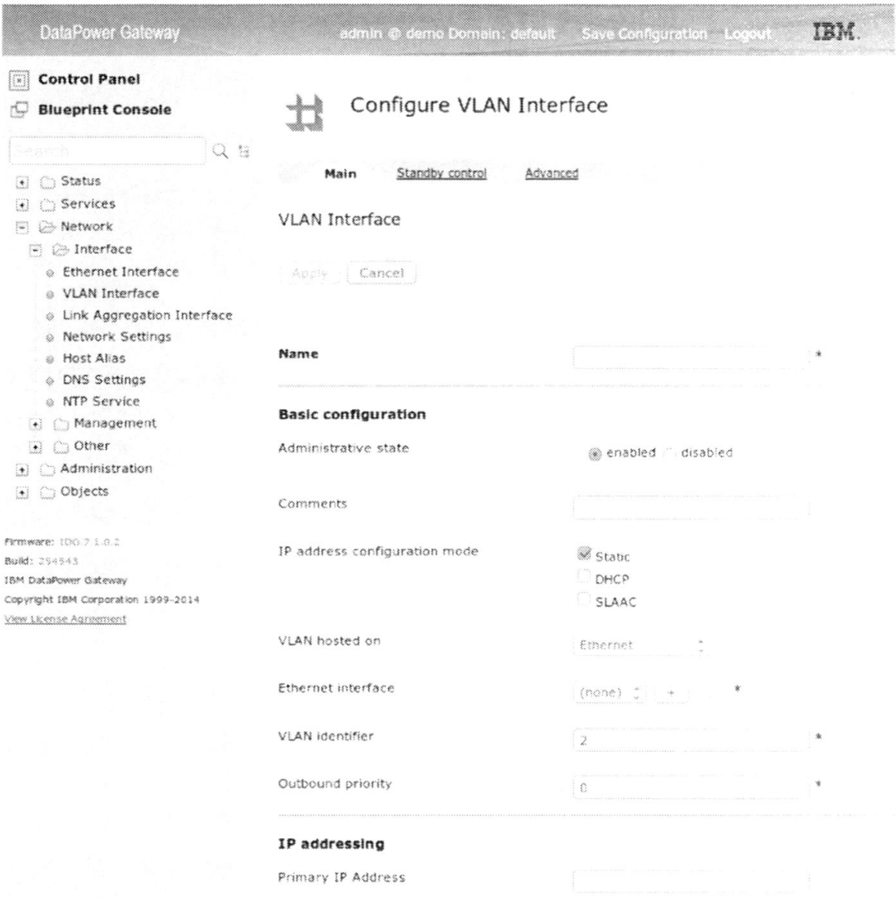

Figure 2-13 Configure VLAN Interface

The MTU for the VLAN (which is on the Advanced tab) can be independently set, but may not be larger than the MTU for the parent interface.

VLAN Interface Status is also available. It is similarly simple, showing only information that can be derived from configuration.

DataPower Networking Scenarios

At this point, we've discussed DataPower, DataPower's network stack, and how to configure it. We've even talked about the theoretical basis of a network stack. Other volumes of the DataPower Handbook detail specific application layer use cases. But between the specific DataPower network configuration and the application layer integration performed by DataPower services there is still an open question: How do I properly integrate DataPower into the network so that it can perform its application-layer role? This is a question with many answers.

The first answer, and the answer we've provided up to now, is "Do what your site network administration and architecture team say." This remains the first best answer because DataPower is usually deployed into environments where these sorts of questions have already been answered from the site network and site security perspectives.

The second answer is that there are still DataPower specific answers to some kinds of network related questions. Questions like "How do I best perform DataPower configuration management when network configuration is not portable?"

The third answer is that you, the DataPower professional, have to be familiar enough with your device that you can effectively work with the network teams supporting the environments where your devices are deployed. You will have to answer their questions correctly so they can help you determine the correct ways to integrate your appliances with the networks they own.

Lastly, this gives us a way to apply what we have already learned, to traverse the networking capabilities of DataPower in-depth for a number of examples.

There is a wide range of ways DataPower can be effectively integrated into a network. There are similarly a wide range of ways that DataPower can be configured in a way that results in undesired side effects or that make it difficult to validate, debug, and maintain. It is your job to be able to tell the former from the latter.

Multiple Security Zones

In one sense, DataPower is extremely capable of being connected to multiple security zones. It is frequently done, and done successfully. Yet there are also multiple security zone examples for which DataPower is not appropriate. Let's look at one of each.

DataPower in the DMZ

DataPower is frequently deployed into the DMZ, where it has an Internet-facing interface and an enterprise-facing interface. There may even be a separate management network (more on that later), which is a third security zone. See Figure 2-14.

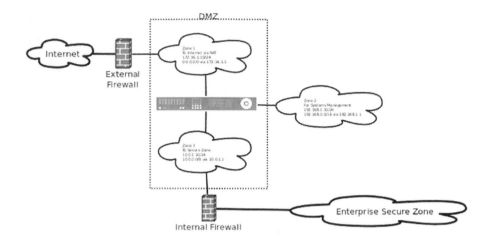

Figure 2-14 DataPower connected three different layer 2 and layer 3 networks

In this scenario, DataPower's one stack and one application execution environment has access to each of the three security zones. A service (such as a front-side protocol handler, WebGUI, or SSH) is bound to one address. The address is specific to an interface. DataPower uses a combination of interface isolation, source address routing, and bind-specific services to ensure that only traffic from the correct zone can access WebGUI or SSH or a front-side protocol handler. The principle applies to each equally; it is DataPower configuration that separates the zones.

Similarly, when DataPower opens a back-side connection or consults LDAP, it picks a source IP address using the appliance-wide route table. This is how DataPower knows that the back-end server is in the trusted enterprise internal network.

This arrangement works well.   The Internet-facing interface has a default gateway. The management interface has its own address in a network that is completely different than the enterprise-facing network.   IP routing can always distinguish among the interfaces.

When Application Configuration is not Enough

The DMZ example above relies on IP routing and application layer configuration (bind addresses) to separate zones 1, 2, and 3 respectively.

What do we mean by application layer configuration in DataPower? We mean everything about the way you configure your DataPower services. Examples are numerous and include local addresses, such as those found on front side handlers and on the SSH, web-management and XML-management services, and URLs that specify back-end services. We mean every user of a host alias or a DNS static host. We mean everything about the way the appliance is configured when it communicates with anything over the network.

How do you know when DataPower configuration is sufficient to separate traffic from different security zones? That is a question that can only be answered by the business on a case-by-case basis.

One example of multiple security zones where businesses frequently decide application layer configuration is insufficient to separate security zones is the use of the same appliance for DMZ and secure zones. Consider:

Acme Enterprises wants to use DataPower in both the DMZ and the secure zone.   Acme realizes that a single appliance is more than capable of handling the load for both zones. Acme further realizes that of course they must have two appliances in each of their two data centers for availability purposes. They do the math—2 appliances per environment x 2 environments per datacenter x 2 datacenters = 8 appliances. Wow, they think. That's a lot of appliances, especially when one could handle the load! Is there any way to reduce the footprint?

The DataPower administrator suggests that the load could still be accommodated by using the same appliance for both the trusted and DMZ zones and still meet the availability requirements of multiple active data centers each with redundant appliances.

The team proceeds with this plan and as they prepare for deployment, they request to open the required ports through the firewall from the trusted zone to the appliance in the DMZ. These ports are the ones required to allow their secure zone traffic reach DataPower. The request was denied.

The team understood that the ports could not be opened because such traffic is not allowed to pass the internal firewall, so they thought about how that might not be required. The idea was presented to connect the single DataPower appliance directly to the secure/trusted zone. This is easy technically— just trunk another VLAN or use another of the plentiful NICs. Yet this was seen by the network team as an even worse option. They proposed extending their DMZ architecture from Figure 2-14 to the Figure shown in 2-15.

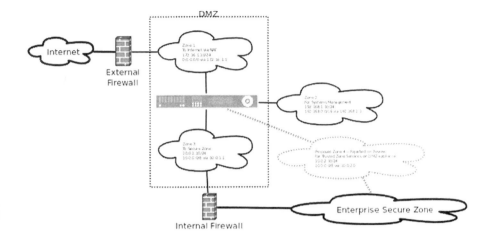

Figure 2-15 Flawed proposed architecture with one DataPower Gateway for both DMZ and trusted zone services.

Why is it a worse option? It is worse because it gives DataPower a path to the trusted zone that does not go through the firewall that sits between the DMZ and the trusted zone. Devices in the DMZ must not do this.

Furthermore, there is no IP routing way to distinguish between connections that DataPower opens in service of the DMZ function and connections DataPower opens in service of the trusted zone function. Therefore, the approach of "use another interface" results in either circumvention of the internal firewall or inappropriate blocking traffic for the internal traffic by the internal firewall.

Eventually, ACME decided to use different options to reduce the size of their deployment while still meeting the security and availability requirements of their business. Or they decided it was worth the added expense of deploying additional DataPower Gateways to meet their original design.

Whichever it was, they learned the importance of involving all stakeholders early in the cycle to avoid situations like this in the future.

One DataPower Configuration for Many Network Environments

Acme has a business need to ensure DataPower application layer configuration is easily portable among its environments. Its environments range from Developer Edition virtual appliances to functional test to performance test to final certification and production. Production itself has multiple appliances in multiple datacenters with configuration that is identical except certain infrastructure is duplicated in each datacenter.

How can Acme minimize the application layer configuration differences between environments?

This is done with a combination of host aliases and DNS configuration with static hosts.

By giving each address on the appliance a host alias and using that as the bind address for each service, the local address is abstracted out of the configuration in one step. This is best done for all appliances in every role on every site.

There are several ways to use DNS settings to abstract out differences between environments.

The first way relies on the nameserver itself to make the distinction. For instance, the name server might say ldap.acme.com is 10.1.2.3 in datacenter 1, 10.2.2.3 in datacenter 2, and 10.100.2.3 internally. These are actually different servers appropriate for different environments but each are appropriate for use by the DataPower service.

Another DNS based way to abstract remote names away from DataPower configuration is to use the same name in different DNS domains. For instance, the DataPower configuration may refer to host 'ldap.' There may be a 'ldap.dc1.acme.com', a 'ldap.dc2.acme.com', and a 'ldap.internal.acme.com'. Appliances in dc1 have 'dc1.acme.com' as their DNS search path. Similarly for appliances in data center 2 and internal.

Lastly, an Acme DataPower developer or test group may need to use a different LDAP server. They want to use the same DataPower configuration but not have to change every occurrence of 'ldap' that refers to a host to 'ldap-next'. For this, they use a DNS static host to map the name 'ldap' to the IP address of ldap-next.

Both host aliases and DNS static hosts were discussed in the previous chapter.

Management Network

It's difficult to talk about a management network because it is not a monolithic concept. The DataPower administrator view of the management network is commonly conceptualized as "the interface with SSH access." This is unlikely how your network administrators think of the management network or even how your DataPower peer administrators think of the management network.

On one hand, a management network is really just a specific example of integrating a single device into multiple security zones. On the other hand, it offers an excellent case study onto which we can further examine not only the nature of a management network but also DataPower and DataPower integration into multiple security zones.

Consider the following views:

1. The management network is a lights-out, out-of-band management network that is used for switch administration, UPS and power system alerts and control, temperature sensors, and similar.

2. The management network is used for all 'meta' functions. It is used for system administration including SSH access, log servers, application level SNMP alerts, SMTP alerts, and the like. DataPower remote configuration or policy may even be loaded from a server in this network.

3. The management interface is DataPower's mgt0 Ethernet interface. The management network is therefore the network that interface mgt0 connects to.

4. The management network is a discrete IP network unto itself, there is no general access to the broader internal network except through a jump server or VPN; access is tightly controlled.

5. The management network is broadly accessible to administrators across the enterprise. It is not a discrete IP network.

This is just a sampling of the way various stakeholders have described their management network. What is important isn't what it is called, but that all the stakeholders in your organization agree about the role of the management network for you. If the network team and facilities teams are a #1 and the DataPower team is a #2 or #3, it's possible the teams may talk right past each other without realizing it.

TIP— DataPower Admin Job Responsibilities

Remember that the DataPower administrator job description includes all the responsibilities of the system administrator, just recast onto the appliance. Among those responsibilities is coordinating with the network administration and architecture teams as well as the facilities and virtualization teams as appropriate. It is your job to ensure DataPower fits properly into the overall solution not only from an application-level integration perspective but also from a physical deployment and network integration perspective.

TIP— Using Other Devices to Check Your Work

Use other devices in the same zone to check your work. If the UNIX or Linux servers in the same zone use SSH on the enterprise-facing network and not on a dedicated management network, then so should DataPower. If the management modules on other servers or chassis are on a dedicated network, then DataPower's IPMI interface should be on that network too.

The way we have phrased the problem may itself be an issue: we talk about the "management network" and the "management interface," but really we have a network (that happens to be used for application-layer data that happens to be associated with device management) and an interface (that happens to be used application-layer data that happens to be associated with device management). The essential nature of these concepts is misplaced—it is the network and the interface that are most important, not the fact that they happen to carry some application-layer data that happens to be "meta" because it is used to manage the appliance.

At this point, you're probably wondering if there is anything at all special about management traffic. There are several answers to this question:

Answer 1: Not really. Only the IPMI LAN channel on mgt0 on rack-mounted form factor appliances is truly special.

Answer 2: It's as special in DataPower as it is in the network topology DataPower is deployed into.

Answer 3: It is special because we frequently change the other interface that might otherwise be used for appliance management, and we don't want to saw off the branch of the tree upon which we are sitting. For example, if routine reconfiguration of eth20 is expected because of standby control, it would not be a good idea to use an address on eth20 management address because doing so could result in no access to SSH and the WebGUI.

The first two answers are strictly security-zone answers. These are by far the most common answers. Answer 3 on the other hand suggests that there may sometimes be a reason to have multiple interfaces on the same network. More on that one in a later section.

From a network security zone analysis, there is no reason to invent a new zone for DataPower management. If there is a requirement for a zone appropriate for DataPower management, it would already be present. Similarly, the absence of such a zone means that DataPower management is not special from a network security zone analysis. Since it is the job of the DataPower administrator to properly integrate the appliance into the network, this means that the DataPower management function should be associated with the most appropriate preexisting network.

But what about "mgt0" and "mgt1," aren't they special? Shouldn't I use them for management?

In terms of being special, only mgt0 truly qualifies. That is because the physical port labeled "mgt0" actually has two different network devices—it is both the DataPower Ethernet interface "mgt0" and the IPMI LAN channel. IPMI offers true lights-out device management.

It is not a requirement and it is not even a best practice to use an address on mgt0 or mgt1 for general-purpose appliance administration. It is not recommended to use mgt0 or mgt1 for transactional traffic. By process of elimination mgt0 or mgt1 may be better suited for DataPower application-level management. Additionally, since mgt0 and mgt1 are not customer replaceable units compared to eth10 through eth17, there may be times when eth10 may fail but mgt0 would not.

Remember, DataPower's management services follow the same rules as all the other services the appliance offers. Their configuration specifies the address they listen upon. The route table specifies how packets are sent. They are not fundamentally special.

Access Control Lists

Despite not being special from a routing and network topology perspective, there are still times when only certain source IP addresses are permissible for management service login. DataPower offers Access Control Lists (ACLs) to solve this problem. With an ACL on the WebGUI, SSH, and xml-mgmt management services only the address ranges permitted by the ACL are allowed to go on and attempt a login.

ACLs are generally available on every DataPower front-side handler as well, so don't discount their use for enforcing other network-level access restrictions on a service-by-service basis.

IP Aliases

There are many situations where it is helpful to have more than one IP address on a network interface, the most common reason is so that different SSL credentials can be used on the same TCP port on the same host. It is no different for DataPower.

TIP— Using the Same Port for Different Certs

One technique that allows a single host or DataPower Gateway to use the same port for different certificates is to *use different IP addresses. That way one front side handler can be bound to <ip1>:443 and another can be bound to <ip2>:443. But there is a newer way, and it is called SNI, or Server Name Indication. DataPower now supports SNI, so this use of IP aliases will get less important as SNI is used more widely.*

But IP aliases (or secondary IP addresses they are called on DataPower) have other uses as well.

They can simulate a multiple security zones in lower environments. In this way, a DataPower developer or tester can have different addresses for different services in the same way as the production appliance is deployed.

They can provide general functional separation even in production. It may be more intuitive to know that address A is for business unit A and address B is for business unit B even if both are in the same security zone. It may also help manage port assignments because it can allow different organizations that share the same DataPower infrastructure to manage their own well-known ports.

Generally a secondary IP address will not be selected as the source address when DataPower initiates a connection. The exception to that rule is when the secondary IP address is in a different subnet than the primary address and the destination is in the same subnet as the secondary address.

Secondary IP addresses are a more lightweight option for multiple addresses in the same layer 2 network than using multiple interfaces. It is also a more standard approach to use multiple addresses on the same interface than to use multiple interfaces in the same layer 2 network.

Multiple Interfaces in the Same Network

It is possible to successfully have multiple interfaces connected to the same layer two or layer three network, but it is not a standard topology because it introduces significant complexities. Anyone considering using multiple interfaces in the same network should think carefully about the range of issues that are likely to come up before deciding to use this topology.

The first complexity it introduces is multiple equivalent routes. There is simply no way around that problem. In order to use multiple interfaces on the same network, one must accept the fact that the implied subnet routes will always be equivalent. This means that if DataPower ever connects to another host in its subnet, then DataPower may, for example, use either mgt0 or eth20 for any of the connections.

In the Management Network section, we mentioned that the management network might be special because "we frequently change the other interface that might otherwise be used for appliance management, and we don't want to saw off the branch of the tree upon which we are sitting."

There are times when operational controls dictate that a network interface must be routinely reconfigured. It may be part of a maintenance window scenario, where standby control must be disabled or the entire interface must be disabled so an external load balancer does not send transactions to an appliance that is undergoing maintenance.

Under such circumstances, it is helpful to have a way to continue to manage the appliance that is more robust than lights-out management but which still allows other network interfaces to be disabled and/or reconfigured.

In this scenario, a dedicated network interface is used for DataPower SSH, WebGUI, and xml-mgmt. It must be acceptable for any same-subnet traffic to use either interface, or for there to be no same-subnet traffic.

Note that in DMZ scenarios, there is frequently no same-subnet traffic, but in enterprise zone scenarios this assumption may not hold.

Routes on the interface used for management must be given a higher metric than routes on the interface used for transactions. This causes routing to favor the transaction interface.

An example of a dedicated management network in conjunction with transaction processing network on the same subnet is shown in Figure 2-16. In this example, the intent is to use 192.168.1.10 for data and 192.168.1.9 for DataPower management traffic. It must be acceptable to us either interface for connections DataPower initiates to the 192.168.1.0/24 subnet.

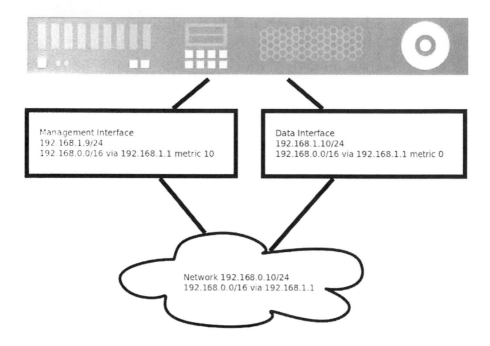

Figure 2-16: Two Interfaces on the Same Subnet

If DataPower's default network setting for source address routing is used, then the "management" interface will be used for both the manager-to-DataPower and the DataPower-to-manager datagrams. If destination routing is used, then the inbound packets will still arrive on the "management" interface, but the outbound packets will leave by the "transaction" interface.

Sometimes we see an "ingress" interface and an "egress" interface on the same network. This is usually done either to increase available bandwidth to the appliance or make it easier to conceptualize the differences between inbound and outbound.

These reasons have historically had a kernel of truth, but they are no longer good reasons to use multiple interfaces on the same network.

If the historic reason was to increase throughput, then the modern answer is either 10Gbit Ethernet or link aggregation.

If the historic reason was conceptual differences, then ask yourself if the actual increase of complexity in the network configuration and the poorer fail-over properties are a price you are willing to pay.

Case Study

Let's look at an example illustrating host aliases, management network, IP aliases, and different network zones.

Let's say ACME enterprises is deploying a group of appliances into the DMZ. The pre-existing DMZ architecture has a lights-out management network, an Internet-facing interface, and an enterprise-facing network. There are two major data flows—customer transactions coming in from the Internet, and partner transactions coming from the enterprise and going out on the Internet. DataPower administration will be performed on the enterprise-facing layer 2/3 network. Different addresses are required for system administration addresses such as SSH access and transactions due to firewall standards.

In order to integrate with this network, the network administration team assigns four addresses to each appliance: acme-dp*-ext for the external or Internet facing network, acme-dp*-ipmi for the lights-out management network, and acme-dp*-int and acme-dp*-mgt on the internal, enterprise-facing network. Only ports 22 (SSH), 161 (SNMP), 5550 (xml-mgmt), and 9090 (WebGUI) of acme-dp1-mgt will be permitted through the firewall from the trusted zone to the appliances in the DMZ. Similarly, acme-dp1-int will be permitted from the DMZ and into the trusted zone for known service addresses, such as for back-end servers, log servers, LDAP authentication and the like. There is external load balancing for both the customer transactions and the partner transactions, and there are multiple appliances in this tier. The load balancers respectively use the acme-dp*-ext and acme-dp*-int addresses.

Since Acme's management and internal addresses are on the same network, and since there is no requirement for routine reconfiguration of that interface, both addresses can be on the same interface.

The management address is added as a secondary IP address so it is not chosen as a source address for connections initiated by the appliance. This helps ensure the firewall can properly recognize connections from the appliance to the trusted zone.

The management services are protected by ACLs that further limit the addresses administrators can use to connect to the appliance. While there is not network level separation between management and internal networks, there are a limited number of valid source IP addresses that are permitted to manage the appliance.

Since this is a rack-mounted appliance that has IPMI LAN channel, mgt0 is dedicated to that and uses the acme-dp*-ipmi address.

The Internet-facing interface gets its single address and default gateway.

A host alias is created for each address used for DataPower services: host-alias "external" for acme-dp*-ext, "internal" for acme-dp*-int, and "management" for acme-dp*-mgt. There is no alias for IPMI since it is only configured in one object and cannot be used as a bind address for services.

There are two different DataPower application domains. Domain "consumer" contains the configuration for the consumer transactions coming from the Internet. Domain "partner" is similarly for partner integration. Front side handlers in the consumer domain use the "external" host-alias for their local address. Front side handlers in the partner domain use the "internal" host-alias for their local address. DataPower's SSH, WebGUI, xml-mgmt, and SNMP services use the "management" host-alias in the default domain.

ACME of course does not have only one environment. There is a second production environment located in another city that shares the same topology. In this environment, everything is the same except the DNS domain and search path is different. Since short address names are used for services throughout the appliance configuration, this allows the same configuration to be able to be used unmodified in the different datacenters.

Not all environments are production. There are "standard" test environment that is topologically similar to production but lacks the redundancy. Additionally there are lower test and development environments which are not topologically similar thus have to be treated somewhat differently.

The standard test environments work the same way as production—that's the point! They are used for final verification, load testing, etc. They rely on support servers and back-ends that are production-like. The DNS short hostname for each of these production-like servers stays the same, but the DNS domain is different.

The lower test and development diverge further. New versions of back-end and support services are tested using DNS static hosts to override the standard pattern. Multiple domains of the same service are bound to different IP addresses to avoid port conflicts on shared appliances. The function development and test environments may only have a single interface. They may only have a single IP address. Yet they too may have the host-alias "external," "internal," and "management" that all refers to the same IP address. These too are fully capable of using any portion of the same services used in the higher level environments.

DataPower Network Topologies

As an astute reader, you'll realize that we managed to get through the "DataPower Network Scenarios" section without ever once mentioning Ethernet, link aggregation, or VLAN. That was no accident. The scenarios are a layer 3 through layer 7 construct, whereas the topologies are layers one and two.

In the scenarios, it does not matter if an IP address is on an Ethernet interface, VLAN interface on Ethernet, link aggregation interface, or a VLAN interface on a link aggregation. It's just an IP address.

Each interface type is a means to deliver IP level configuration. It is also the definition of layer 2 connectivity. That is all it is—every function that can be done on an Ethernet can also be done on a VLAN or an aggregation.

That is not to say that every topology is equivalent. Some are demonstratively better than others. Some are well-suited to one platform but ill-suited to another. Each will provide layer 2 connectivity. But the technologies and the way they are deployed together result in different failure modes, and failure modes are critical to understand and control in production environments.

In this section, we endeavor to analyze a number of network topologies. We point out the tasks they are well-suited for, those they are ill-suited for, and where possible a better replacement topology.

But our suggestions will be fundamentally flawed. We cannot know about the environments you are deploying your appliances into. There are factors outside DataPower that trump any of the general recommendations and analysis we can make here. It is your role to learn the lessons and apply the general knowledge to your specific networks and to work with those responsible for the safety and well being of your network to come up with an approach that works for all.

Lastly, we will assume that no matter the topology or network interfaces chosen that routing is deterministic.

One Ethernet Interface

This is where everyone should start. Whether it's to accept the license on a new or reinitialized appliance or the beginning of a new project, starting with a single Ethernet interface is a good move.

On DataPower Virtual Edition appliances that only connect to a single security zone, one virtual Ethernet interface is a perfectly acceptable production configuration. Especially if the hypervisor is providing link aggregation to the physical network.

If DataPower is connecting to more than one security zone, one interface won't be enough. On virtual, consider multiple (virtual) Ethernet interfaces or using VLANs.

One Ethernet interface on a physical appliance cannot be resilient to the loss of a single switch or cable. Consider using a link aggregation or having an availability model that treats the loss of the one link as the loss of the appliance.

IPMI LAN Channel

A rack-mounted appliance using the port mgt0 exclusively for IPMI is a high-quality pattern. Note that in this example, there would be no DataPower Ethernet configuration for mgt0, only ipmi-lan-channel.

In this sense, IPMI does not count as a DataPower Ethernet interface because it is not used by DataPower itself, only the management board.

It is possible use mgt0 for both IPMI and DataPower Ethernet or DataPower non-LACP link aggregation. But because of the complexities this introduces, it may be preferable to dedicate mgt0 to IPMI instead.

More Than One Ethernet Interface

On the virtual platform, using one DataPower Ethernet interface per security zone to integrate into an existing vswitch standard configuration is a high-quality pattern.

On physical appliances, patterns such as this are not highly available. Consider using link aggregation with VLANs instead if the appliance should be able to tolerate the loss of a link.

One Ethernet Interface with VLANs

This is another case where it can be a high-quality production deployment on virtual DataPower but is less well-suited for physical appliances.

If the vswitch is configured to trunk VLANs and the vswitch provides link-layer availability, then this is a high-quality production deployment topology.

However, on the physical appliances the loss of the single Ethernet interface causes the loss of the entire device from production.

While the loss of the device is bad, external load balancing technologies can frequently detect and recover from this scenario easily.

In that sense, it is preferable to lose an entire appliance than it is to lose part of an appliance. A partially down appliance can't successfully process transactions, but still it tries. In trying, every transaction it attempts fails. A failed transaction is forever—it can't be undone. It is a visible sign of the outage to customers. This is the thing to avoid. If instead we let a different appliance process the transaction, customers would not see any sign of trouble.

Furthermore, a completely down appliance is easy for load balancers to detect. This is discussed in depth in the section "Multiple Highly Available Interfaces are Less Available Than One Highly Available Interface."

Failure mode is important. Here we have a choice of failure modes. Would we rather fail in a way that allows transactions to be processed by a broken node or in a way that causes a broken node to be automatically taken out of production? Clearly the latter. If one Ethernet interface fails and it causes the entire node to be taken out of production, that is better than having one Ethernet interface fail and having the node left in production but unable to successfully process transactions. Because of this, a better topology on physical appliances is likely link aggregation with VLAN. However, the recommendation is tempered by the availability strategy for the network and applications as a whole.

More Than One Ethernet Interfaces with VLANs

In post v7 firmware, there are a vanishingly small number of scenarios where something like this should be done.

On Virtual, where the hypervisor connects to two different physical networks comes to mind, but then one has to question why those two networks were separate in the first place. Perhaps in some preproduction scenarios it may happen.

Perhaps using multiple Ethernet interfaces was done as a way to spread load over several different interfaces, in which case it is better to use one link aggregation interface with VLANs.

Perhaps it was a historical artifact of DataPower Standby Control where there was a limitation of a single standby control group per DataPower Ethernet interface, but that limitation was lifted in v7.

Despite all this, if that truly is the way the network and security architecture expects all devices in this zone to be configured, DataPower should be similarly configured. Remember, the overriding principle is that DataPower should be configured to match the expectations of the network, not the other way around. Do talk with the network architecture team about the failure mode. Do understand why it is the way it is. But at the end of the day, DataPower matches the network. If the network has to change because of appropriate feedback to the network and security architecture teams, then so be it, but in the meantime DataPower still matches the network, and at the end of the process, DataPower is changed to continue to match the corrected network.

One Link Aggregation Interface

If a physical form factor appliance is only connected to a single network or security zone and the connection is required to tolerate the loss of a single Ethernet link, or the a single Ethernet interface does not provide enough bandwidth, using a single link aggregation interface is just the ticket.

If there are multiple networks or security zones, first consider handling them by adding VLANs atop a single link aggregation interface.

In scenarios where the single link aggregation interface may need to be frequently reconfigured in support of a business process, consider avoiding that by using multiple link aggregation interfaces or a single link aggregation interface with an Ethernet interface.

There are also times when link aggregation in DataPower should not be used.

For virtual DataPower, any link aggregation should be performed by the hypervisor so it would not appear in DataPower configuration. Use a single virtual Ethernet interface in this case.

If the network topology does not explicitly support link aggregation, or the network team has not fully vetted the link aggregation configuration, link aggregation in DataPower should be avoided. Use a single Ethernet interface in this case.

Using a single link aggregation interface is a high quality pattern when there is only one network for a physical DataPower appliance to integrate with. In these situations, we suggest also using IPMI LAN Channel for lights-out management.

One Link Aggregation Interface with VLANs

This is the gold-standard of the link aggregation topologies. It should be the first choice link-aggregation topology when physical DataPower is required to connect to multiple networks.

It is the gold standard because it fails the most gracefully; it avoids unnecessary partitioning of available bandwidth; and it provides layer 2 separation on par with what is provided in the switching topology.

However, there are still times when it should not be used.

Bandwidth sharing is only applicable when using LACP, yet there may still be sufficient bandwidth for this pattern if using 10Gb interfaces. If neither LACP nor 10Gbit is an option, a business decision to will have to be made which of the other less-desirable options should be used. You will have to make tradeoffs, so careful study of the overall properties of the topology will have to be performed. Refer to the discussion of multiple link aggregation interfaces, because it may be better to use multiple link aggregations than to use multiple Ethernet interfaces.

TIP— Don't Change the Native VLAN

*Avoid changes to the native (untagged) VLAN. By doing so, each of the VLANs can be changed independently. If there is standby control or other re-configuration performed on the link aggregation itself, it will disrupt the VLANs atop the link aggregation. One easy way to avoid changing the link aggregation interface is to **not** use it for IP configuration.*

One Link Aggregation Interface with Ethernet Interface

This topology is useful when there are two networks DataPower must integrate with that have different availability or complexity properties.

For instance, if production traffic is on a network that offers link aggregation but the separate management network does not, the only possibility that meets business requirements and integrates with the existing network is to use a link aggregation for the data network and Ethernet for the management.

This pattern is also a helpful intermediate step to the full deployment of link aggregation. Even if the ultimate goal is to have full redundant networking for every DataPower service, using a time-tested and well-understood Ethernet interface for management in conjunction with a link aggregation for data offers a way to incrementally achieve that goal while preserving management access to the appliance.

More Than One Link Aggregation Interface

More than one link aggregation interface should primarily be used when DataPower is integrating with more than one layer one network. In other words, there are two physically distinct networks that DataPower must connect to and link aggregation is required.

Additionally, scenarios where frequent operations are performed on link aggregation interface may call for a second link aggregation interface to be deployed for robust management access. The use of standby control directly on the link aggregation interface may be one such scenario; but moving the standby control to a VLAN may be a better choice.

Multiple link aggregation interfaces may also be helpful in lower environments when testing interface configuration and standby control to permit multiple scenarios to be run on a single appliance at the same time.

In the absence of physically separated networks, patterns that involve production transactions that require more than one link aggregation interface to be used should be avoided.

More Than One Link Aggregation Interface with VLANs

There are scenarios where an approach like this makes sense, but the frequency is diminishing.

The standard advice—match DataPower to the existing network applies.

Using 1Gbit Ethernet interfaces in an aggregation that is used for management and all the 10Gbit Ethernet interfaces in an aggregation that has VLANs and is used for data may meet business requirements. But as we discussed earlier, why not use another VLAN for management?

If we're talking about several aggregations each with VLANs, then we're likely talking mostly contrived scenarios and not integration into production networks. It is difficult to imagine a production scenario where multiple layer one networks that DataPower has to integrate into using multiple link aggregation interfaces.

Virtual Ethernet Interfaces and Virtual Switches

When DataPower is itself virtual, its Ethernet interfaces are also virtual. And the "switch" that they connect to is most commonly also virtual.

All these virtual components nevertheless make up a very real part of the network topology.

The basic availability and performance properties of the DataPower network interfaces are wholly dependent on the availability and performance properties of the hypervisor and its vswitch.

We've mentioned that DataPower link aggregation is not used on Virtual. The reason for this comes down to the nature of the virtual Ethernet interface. It simply is the hypervisor. With copper or fiber Ethernet cables, it is easy to understand what it might mean for one to fail. If a hypervisor's Ethernet interface fails, it means the hypervisor itself has failed—there is nothing that can be done to recover from this situation except use a different hypervisor.

The hypervisor and vswitch present one view to DataPower, this view that looks-like-Ethernet-but-is-not. But the vswitch is also responsible for its uplink—where the vswitch plugs into a real Ethernet switch through the hosts' network adapters.

This is where once again it is easy to imagine the failed copper or fiber uplink.

The solution to this problem is the same as it is for other physical devices—use link aggregation! And that is exactly how the problem is solved—the hypervisor uses its own link aggregation as the uplinks for the vswitch which provides connectivity to the guests, such as DataPower. DataPower's link aggregation is not used.

Multiple highly available interfaces are less available than one highly available interface

We've mentioned several times that it is better to have a single aggregation and use VLANs to separate traffic than it is to use multiple aggregations. As this is a counter-intuitive assertion, it's worth unpacking it further.

Let's consider two different topologies, A and B.

Topology A has two aggregations each with two links. Both aggregations are required in order to process transactions— perhaps in a straightforward DMZ scenario where we have an ingress interface facing the Internet and an egress interface facing the enterprise.

Topology B has one aggregation with four links and two VLANs. Both VLANs are required in order to process transactions.

Let's also assume that there is a load balancer in front of the group of appliances, and that it can detect if the front side handler is down with the standard TCP half-open health check. Or let's assume that DataPower Self-Balancing is on the Internet-facing interface. The results are the same in either case.

Now, let's see what the result is when different network interfaces, or groups of network interfaces, or switches are lost.

Table 2-4 Results when network components are lost.

Number of Lost Links	Topology A 2 Aggs Available Bandwidth	Topology A Complication	Topology B 1 Agg + VLAN Available Bandwidth	Topology B Complication
0	100%	None	100%	None
1+0	50%	None	75%	None
0+1	50%	Bottleneck	75%	None
1+1	50%	None	50%	None
2+0	0%	Down	50%	None
0+2	0%	Transaction Failures	50%	None
2+1	0%	Down	25%	None
1+2	0%	Transaction Failures	25%	None
2+2	0%	Down	0%	Down

As you can see, there are no scenarios in which topology A, the one with two aggregations, has better behavior in the face of adversity than topology B. Fewer broken links result in more bandwidth loss. There are more failure modes – some of which cannot be easily detected and mitigated through other techniques.

Look at the complications for both failure modes. Not only are more ways that topology A can result in an unavailable appliance, but there are two different failure modes that it can experience which are not experienced in topology B. First is that using two aggregations can introduce a bottleneck if one link of the back-side aggregation is down. Bottlenecks can increase latency and memory pressure on the appliance. The second is that it can try to process transactions even though it lacks the layer 2 network connectivity to advance the transaction. It can never reach the back-end server so the best that can happen is a timeout and transaction failure. This too does not happen when using a single aggregation.

The result of this analysis is quite portable. They can be easily extended to side calls, or situations where bandwidth is not symmetrically used.

When it comes to the number of dependencies, fewer is better. Fewer link aggregations leads to fewer dependencies which leads to fewer failure modes which leads to both more availability and more savings.

Summary

The rule is still to work with your network, security, virtualization, and every other team appropriate to each environment you deploy DataPower Gateways into.

The difference is that now, you have a better understanding of how DataPower integrates into each network in your deployments. You know when to use link aggregation, and when not. You know about layer two integration—how and when to use link aggregation, VLANs, and Ethernet. You know how to talk with the network team about those integrations. You know how virtualization relates to the switch topology and how that in turn relates to DataPower Virtual Edition. You know how IP routing works and how IP routing relates to host configuration in general and DataPower configuration specifically.

You are now well equipped to understand the most fundamental integration that there is to be made between the DataPower Gateway and your enterprise network. It is only by understanding how DataPower integrates into your network that you can understand, troubleshoot, and advise others on how DataPower should integrate with higher level services in the enterprise.

Chapter 3

DataPower High Availability

Application Layer Availability and DataPower

The point of scrutinizing interface level availability is to build an application that is in its entirety highly available. This means that the application must continue to operate acceptably in every scenario from regional complete power and communications failure to a broken server or fiber.

This is no small task, yet it is achievable if everyone does their part. And for that to be possible, the teammates must agree on what "their part" is.

Let's start with a basic outline of the prototypical global availability strategy.

Datacenter Availability and Global Load Balancing

Assume there are three datacenters. Each datacenter has 50% capacity, meaning that there is 150% capacity built into the system. One datacenter can be offline for maintenance or disaster and the application itself still has 100% capacity.

It cannot be that one datacenter is more important than the others—any of them could fail. It cannot be that there is a dependency on any other datacenter for any transaction.

The availability strategy cannot be to forward transactions out of a failed datacenter. After all, that datacenter is now cold and dark, there is nothing capable of forwarding out of such a datacenter.

This places some critical limits on the way the DataPower appliance is configured. To start with, Load Balancer groups and DNS static hosts should only refer to systems in the same availability zone. But the problem is much more pervasive than—it touches on every bit of configuration that references every other host that DataPower uses.

Nor is it limited to the data processing path. Log servers, SMTP servers and utility services must also be limited to the same availability zone.

As the DataPower owner, you are responsible for ensuring that your device plays its part and does not drag in unmitigated dependencies. The only way to know if a dependency is mitigated or not, or if it is in the same availability zone or not is to understand the nature of each and every dependency.

If that sounds like a big responsibility, you're right—it is.

While it is your job to stay in the same availability zone, it is the job of someone else to ensure the zones themselves failover properly.

This could be a large topic in and of itself, but the abbreviated version is that there are only two technologies that are capable of directing transactions away from a failed datacenter. Those technologies are Domain Name Service and Dynamic Routing.

Of those, DNS based approaches have won in the enterprise networking space. A number of vendors offer products to help with this problem, but they all work in roughly the same way—by answering a portion of the DNS requests for the same name with different IP addresses. Dynamic routing works by leveraging the Internet's core routing protocols such as OSPF (Open Shortest Path First) or BGP (Border Gateway Protocol) to advertise that there are two or more places on the Internet that have the same IP address.

DNS based approaches rely on the intrinsically redundant model of the DNS system where there are multiple well-known authoritative servers for each name. Then, when a client resolves www.example.com the enhanced name server ensures that it answers with only IP addresses that are in currently-available datacenters.

Because of the way these DNS based approaches work, it can be difficult to know if the dependent server you are using is in the local availability zone or not. This is one more example of how good communication is required for good teamwork—the only way to know is to ask.

Commonly the IP address the DNS based load balancer (or Global Load Balancer) provides is itself a Virtual IP Address, or VIP, that is used for a second tier of load balancing.

The global load balancer is the first tier of a standard load balancing architecture—its job is to get IP traffic from clients to a local load balancer which is the second tier of load balancing. Why is it coarse? How does it work? Let us take a closer look at how DNS resolution works in the context of a global load balancer. This is shown in Figure 3-1.

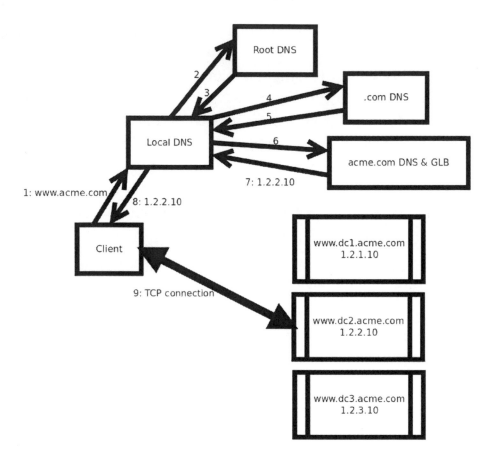

Figure 3-1 DNS lookup process with a Global Load Balancer

In Figure 3-1, you can see that the client requests www.acme.com from the local DNS server. If the local DNS server has an empty cache, it might have to ask the root server (2), await that response (3), ask the .com server (4), and await that response (5), Now it can ask of the acme.com authoritative name server what the address is for "www.acme.com," which it does in (6). The local DNS server is unaware that the acme.com DNS server is integrated with a global load balancer, so when the acme.com DNS responds in (7) with the answer, there is nothing special about it. When the local DNS server responds in (8) with the answer, it too sees nothing special about the answer. The client then connects to the address supplied, which we know happens to be in Datacenter two as seen in (9).

The way DNS based global load balancing works means that there are considerations for application owners. Especially for DataPower.

There is no guarantee that a client will always be directed to the same datacenter. Global load balancers can use heuristics to try to minimize clients from switching from one datacenter to another, but it is impossible to prevent. Eventually DNS records expire and the client has to look up the address again. The global load balancer might respond with a different answer. The client might be in a different place and receive a different cached entry.

Because there is no way to ensure that the same datacenter will process the same client, there must be a strategy for dealing with clients who switch from one datacenter to another. Oftentimes this strategy involves logic in DataPower. Global load balancing is a coarse instrument. The very thing that makes it well suited for disaster conditions—that it is not in-line with transactions—make it ill-suited for fine-grained local load balancing because the DNS request volume at the acme.com DNS server are only loosely correlated to actual transaction volume each datacenter receives. One answer of "1.2.2.10" may result in no client connections or it may result in hundreds of thousands, there is simply no way to know ahead of time.

The responsibility for the global load balancing infrastructure usually lies with the load balancing, DNS, or network team. But the DataPower Gateway team may well be responsible for the application layer affinity.

Local or In-Line Load Balancing

The global load balancer gives the client an IP address. That IP address is itself often a VIP, a Virtual IP Address that is owned by a local load balancer.

The local load balancer is in-line with traffic. It would do no good to have a local load balancer that was itself a single point of failure, so these are normally redundant. The failure of a local load balancer is normally mitigated by placing the local load balancer in a highly available group.

The local load balancer knows which actual servers are capable of handling specific requests. In the simplest case, a request is a TCP connection and the local load balancer is aware of protocol headers from the TCP/UDP port and lower.

DataPower appliances have to be integrated into this environment. For DataPower to play its part in delivering a highly-available service, there must be something that provides this capability.

That something can either be performed by the network or load balancing teams responsible for the availability zone, or it can be provided by DataPower's own self-balancing feature.

Either way, there is coordination. If DataPower is performing local load balancing, then the coordination will be with the global load balancing team. On the other hand, if a stand-alone local load balancer is used, that team will need to know about every member DataPower tier and every service the DataPower tier offers.

Additionally, either way there is process coordination. Operationally there must be procedures to add or remove nodes from a tier. There must be automated availability criteria agreed upon. Each tier must know just enough about its neighbors so that effective collaboration is possible.

Application / Session Aware Load Balancing

We won't go into too much detail here about application layer load balancing here except to say that there are a great many configuration points in DataPower that deal directly with this topic.

This is part of what DataPower does!

DataPower looks deeply into the application layer and determines the correct "application layer routing" for the transaction. Part of that decision process is the concept of session and which application and which application version should handle a specific request.

Intra-Enterprise Availability

Each component in an enterprise application topology will have its own availability strategy. We normally think of this in terms of the transaction flow—perhaps client requests flowing to the highly available datacenter by way of global load balancing, then to a load balancer and through a highly available proxy tier and perhaps through a tier of highly available application servers and finally artifacts resting on highly available systems of record.

As a first pass, this is not bad! Sure sounds highly available, right?

Except it has not accounted for the side-calls that are also required for each tier to both successfully advance the transaction and in order for transactions to advance through the system. Put another way, it's not just a first-order analysis of nodes directly on the transaction path that matters. It's an n-order analysis of nodes on the transaction path, the things those nodes depend upon, and the things those nodes depend on, and so on. Everything counts!

No one person can know all the things everyone depends upon—modern IT is far too complicated for that. But that does not mean that you can't plan on inter-operating properly with the availability strategies used by other services and tiers. It simply means that for every external dependency—be it DNS, LDAP, back-end servers, log servers, etc you understand its availability strategy in so far as it affects the DataPower configuration.

Take DNS as an example. Names have to be resolved. If names cannot be resolved, transactions will (eventually) fail. When a name cannot be resolved it results in significant latency.

What is the availability strategy for DNS in your own availability zone? Should you use a single name server secure in the knowledge that there is a local load balancer fronting it?

Should you use multiple name servers knowing that they take longer to fail?

Do you need to use DNS servers at all? If a service's name is itself a global load balanced name, then perhaps the answer is no and DNS static hosts could be used to eliminate this dependency. Although that would add a different dependency on the potential that the IP address for the service changes and DataPower is unaware.

The DNS caching policy for the service is related to the overall availability as well. In general, longer cache times result in fewer issues for brief application outages. Longer cache times also result in less load on the dependent service. However, longer cache times also result in slower response to change and possibly stale data in the cache. As such, the recommendation is to make cache times as long as they can be to still meet the business requirements for flexibility and as short as they can be otherwise.

For DNS, the cache times are set by the server. But we're talking about names inside the enterprise, so the broader team has the ability to set this policy appropriately for all stakeholders.

DataPower is not unique in this way. Every node in the application graph similarly has to manage its dependencies. However, DataPower's frequent position as a highly-connected core node makes DataPower central to the analysis.

Please don't make the mistake of thinking about this as a DNS specific problem. Absolutely anything can be an external dependency. The DataPower config or XML policy that is cached and fetched from a web-server. Log servers. Side calls. Absolutely anything.

Similarly don't make the mistake of thinking that it takes an outage to impact the application health. Slow response will delay transactions which will increase memory footprints and concurrent transactions. Think about all these things when evaluating the services you provide and the services you depend upon.

Lastly, while this advice applies to DataPower and is delivered in a DataPower specific context, it applies equally to any implementation.

DataPower Availability—Standby Control and Self-Balancing

DataPower itself offers both failover and local load balancing with virtual IP addresses.

Standby Control is DataPower's failover feature. It allows two or more appliances in the same broadcast domain to share the responsibility of service availability by ensuring the availability of a VIP.

Self-balancing extends standby control with local load balancing. With self-balancing, a group of appliances are load balanced (clustered) by themselves without requiring a dedicated external load balancer. Self-balancing is only available on appliances with the Application Optimization licensed feature.

Standby Control Theory

In order for standby control to work, each group member must be able to communicate with each other group member, the mechanism for taking over the VIP must be robust, and each member must know its part. Let's discuss each of those in turn.

Standby control communication is performed over IP multicast to the all-routers address. This is a multicast address that cannot be routed. Under normal conditions, each and every group member must be able to see multicast datagrams from every other group member. This is only possible if every group member is in the same broadcast domain.

VIP Mechanics

With standby control, the VIP is special in that every group member in some sense must have the VIP and any group member may be the current owner of the VIP.

Whenever standby control is configured, an interface with the "-vip" suffix is created and each VIP is placed on that interface. As far as the stack on the appliance is concerned, it owns the VIP, it simply does not advertise that it owns the VIP. That part is conditional on the state of the standby control group.

When a group member takes over VIP ownership, it must have a technique to bring all VIP traffic into itself. It does this with a gratuitous ARP. A gratuitous ARP, also called an unsolicited ARP or grat ARP, is a broadcast ARP frame that forces each node on the network to update its ARP cache. In this way, every IP host that has a cached MAC address to IP address mapping is forced by standards to update its cache. This causes every station that has recently transmitted IP datagrams to the VIP to immediately start using the new station.

If a station does not have the MAC address to VIP address mapping in its ARP cache, it properly ignores the grat ARP. However, if it later needs to send a datagram to the VIP, it will use ARP to determine the MAC address of the VIP. The answer it receives will only be the current owner of the VIP, and this act of performing the lookup will populate the ARP cache such that subsequent grat ARPs will be honored.

Unless the grat ARPs are not honored. Many devices can be configured to disregard grat ARPs. This is generally useful when the layer 2 network itself is not trustworthy. Think of hotel or coffee shop guest networks for examples of these networks. Fortunately, the set of locations one wants to deploy DataPower and the set of locations where grat ARP is contraindicated do not overlap much if at all. Nevertheless, if one uses DataPower's standby control feature, one must ensure that the stations in the directly-attached broadcast domain honor gratuitous ARP. Including and especially the router.

Standby Control Mechanics

Now that all the appliances are in the same broadcast domain, how do they decide which should be active? For that, DataPower uses a protocol based on HSRP—Hot Standby Router Protocol. A great deal of information is available on HSRP, including RFC 2281. In fact, Standby Control groups must not conflict with any HSRP groups used by the routers.

The way standby control works may seem a bit convoluted—and it is—but keep in mind that it works this way in order to assure proper operation under failure conditions. What happens when communication among nodes is lost? What happens when it is regained? If at any time the group members disagree, the potential exists for all transactions to the group to fail. Additionally, any time the owner of the VIP fails, there is an interruption in transaction processing. With only standby control, every in-flight connection is broken. With self-balancing it isn't as bad, but it still has cost.

The most interesting HSRP states for standby control are Active, Standby, Speak, and Listen.

Think of the Active member as king or queen. Once the queen ascends the throne, she is there for life. There are no normal circumstances which will cause her to relinquish the throne. The queen regularly announces herself to the group so that all her subjects know she is in charge. Only the Active member advertises ownership of the VIP.

The Standby member is next-in-line for the throne. Let's call him the crown prince. If the queen dies the crown prince becomes Active, he becomes king.   The crown prince also routinely advertises his status—everyone in the kingdom knows he is next in line for the throne.

In steady state, the remaining group members are royalty in Listen state.

If it ever comes to pass that there is no one next in line for the crown, a member of royalty "Speaks" announcing his claim to that position. He does this even though he has no way of knowing if he has the best claim to the thrown. He therefore looks out for competing announcements that a higher-ranking prince is either claiming the throne or has claimed the throne. If he sees these announcements, he goes back to Listen.

Similarly, if a royal member ever sees that a lower-ranking individual is next in line for the throne, he speaks. In doing so, he will ascend to crown-prince status, displacing the old crown prince who willingly relinquishes his claim.

Let's see how this works with an example. Let's start with royals Ann, Blake, Christine, and David. Their rank is alphabetical.

They all begin in Listen. After a respectable wait, Christine speaks, announcing her intention to become crown prince.

They all see Christine's notice, but Ann and Blake both are of higher status so they both speak in response. Christine relinquishes her claim when she sees Ann and Blake's announcements.

Blake however also sees Ann's notice, so he too relinquishes his claim to crown prince and moves back to Listen.

After a time, Ann moves into Standby, then after a time into Active. At this point she is officially queen.

Once Ann is no longer in Standby, the process repeats. One of the remaining royal family Speaks, sending notices of intent to claim crown prince. Perhaps this time it is Blake who speaks first. The remaining members see that Blake has a better claim than their own, so Christine and David both remain in Listen.

At this point, the royals have successfully sorted themselves and steady state is achieved. Years pass. Ann is posting her queenly notices, Blake is posting his crown-princely notices. All is well in the kingdom. Alas, something happens to Ann. Perhaps she is beset by illness. Perhaps the road was impassable thus her notices were not delivered. Perhaps she is rebooted or has lost connectivity. Whatever the cause, her queenly notices are not delivered.

When that happens, Blake becomes king. After Blake becomes king, Christine and/or David Speak. Perhaps this time David speaks first, Christine sees that notice and speaks herself, David then goes back to listen and Christine ascends to Standby or crown-princess status.

Ann sees none of this, for reasons we do not know.

However, after a time, Ann returns. There are two different versions of this tale.

In one version, Ann never stopped being queen. One part of her kingdom was separated from her, so they did not see her ongoing announcements. This is similar to a network bifurcation scenario, and Ann is still Active.

In another version, such as when Ann relinquished her throne or otherwise stopped governing for a period of time, Ann comes back in Listen state. This is similar to an intentional yield of standby, reconfigure of the interface, or reboot.

If Ann comes back in Listen, she knows her reign has been interrupted, but she still has higher standing than other royal members. She sees that Christine is crown princess and speaks. Christine sees that Ann is higher priority and moves to Listen. Ann then moves through Speak state to Standby. Here she stops—there is already a ruler, and she does not wish to interrupt such a productive rein.

If, however, the split kingdoms are rejoined and Ann is still Active, then she will remain queen. Blake sees Ann's messages and rejoices in the return of his beloved queen. He then speaks. Christine sees Blake's notice, and since Blake has higher status, she moves from Standby to Listen, as Blake eventually becomes the acknowledged crown prince—he's in Standby.

There many more stories we could tell about the adventures of these four. The combinations are not quite endless, but they are significant. A few important things to remember:

- Every node must be able to fulfill every role. Each node is equivalent.

- There is no such thing as "primary" or "secondary." Under normal operation in a two-node deployment the first in always wins. Primary and secondary are different than active and standby because one would always expect the primary node to be active if it is healthy. This is simply not the way it works, and attempts to force DataPower into this model are ill-advised and counter-productive. See the discussion of "preempt" below.

- There are excellent resources available to further understand the states Standby Control uses. Among our favorite is "http://www.cisco.com/c/en/us/support/docs/ip/h ot-standby-router-protocol-hsrp/10583-62.html" for its state transition diagram and description of states.

- Wireshark   decodes   DataPower's   HSRP appropriately.

Lastly, we've not discussed it, but 'preempt' should never be used. When preempt is used, the highest priority appliance always becomes active. In order for this to happen, ownership of the VIP must transfer. If ownership of the VIP transfers, transactions are affected. It is an expensive operation and one that should be avoided. Think of "preempt" as a two outages for the price of one "feature."

Self-Balancing Theory

Self-Balancing is built atop Standby Control. Self-balancing is standby control with few different elements added.

When a self-balancing standby control group member is Active, that group member is also the 'distributor.' It is the distributor's responsibility to load balancing incoming connections by forwarding packets to the other members. Each group member knows how to be the distributor, but only the active member actually performs the forwarding.

Each group member knows about all the services provided by each other group member. Similarly, each group member knows if each other group member is no longer available. This is negotiated with multicast IP on the same address and port combination as is used for standby control.

The distributor fundamentally operates on layers 2-5. It looks at Ethernet frames, IP headers, and TCP headers to distribute the packets that make up TCP connections to the group members as appropriate. The distributor does not terminate the connection—self-balancing is not a proxy, it is a load balancing router. The distributor changes only the MAC layer headers to deliver an identical IP datagram to the appropriate target appliance.

Each target appliance sees the incoming datagram as it was seen by the distributor. The source IP address, source TCP port, destination IP address, and destination IP port are all unchanged by the forwarding process. Each target appliance responds to a client connection identically in the self-balanced case as the native-address case. There is literally no difference as far as the target appliance is concerned.

Let's follow a TCP syn as it flows from the Client to the Router to the Distributor and to the Target, then the syn+ack as it returns back to the client. This is demonstrated in Figure 3-2.

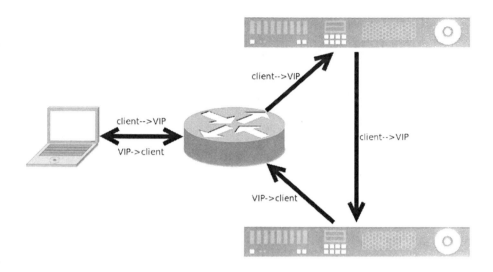

Figure 3-2 Self-Balancing IP Flow

The TCP syn is sent by the client and reaches the router. The router has the VIP in its ARP cache, and uses that to forward the syn to the distributor, which is the top appliance in Figure 3-2. The distributor decides which appliance should handle this new connection and forwards the syn to the target. The target appliance responds with syn+ack to the client, looks up in its route table how it should reach the client, and finds the router. The target has the router in its ARP cache, so uses that to send the syn+ack to the router, which forwards it to the client.

Notice that the routing was asymmetric. On the inbound path, the packet went Client to Router to Distributor to Target. On the outbound path, the packet went Target to Router to Client. The return traffic does not go through the distributor.

Network Requirements

In order to use standby control and self-balancing, there are a number of requirements. While we have touched on most of these separately, calling out all the network requirements in one place is still helpful.

- You must have one or more Virtual IP addresses. The VIPs must be in the same broadcast domain as the standby control group.

- You must honor gratuitous ARP on all stations on the broadcast domain, including the router. Put another way, gratuitous ARP must be sufficient to effect a takeover.

- You must be able to forward IP packets to other group members.

- IP Multicast must work properly among all group members.

- The Standby Control Group number must not conflict with any other standby control groups or HSRP groups that are deployed on the network.

- You must not use the same Standby Control group on multiple network interfaces on the same DataPower gateway.

TIP— Group Number Confirmation

Determine if the group number is used by both talking with the network team and by taking a packet capture. Group one is most commonly used by routers, so DataPower should avoid that group.

Using Standby Control and Self-Balancing

A Standby control group is configured on the "Standby control" tab of the Ethernet Interface, Link Aggregation Interface, or VLAN Interface. Standby control is configured in the same way no matter the interface type.

On the appropriate interface, navigate to the Standby control tab and turn Enable standby control on and Enable self-balancing on. The panel is shown in Figure 3-3.

Configure Ethernet Interface

Main   **Standby control**   Advanced

Ethernet Interface: eth1 [up]

[Apply] [Cancel] [Delete] [Undo]

Start packet capture | Stop packet ca

Basic properties for standby control

Enable standby control	● on ○ off
Group number	224 *
Primary virtual IP address	1.2.3.4 *
Enable preemption	○ on ● off *
Secondary virtual IP addresses	(empty) / [add]
Priority	100 *
Enable self-balancing	● on ○ off *
Distribution algorithm	Round robin *

Advanced properties for standby control

Authentication data	0x5841333500000000 *
Hello timer	3 Seconds *
Hold timer	10 Seconds *

Figure 3-3 Configure Ethernet Interface Standby Control tab

The group number must be unique both on the appliance and in the network. That is to say that the same group number must not be used on both Ethernet interface eth10 and VLAN 200. And the same group number must not be used on the same network for both a DataPower standby control group and a router HSRP group.

The primary virtual IP address is the VIP. It must be native to the layer 2 network, but it need not be in the same subnet as the interface's primary IP address. For instance, the VIP might be publicly routable 1.2.3.4 and the primary IP address might be 10.2.3.4/24, and this is perfectly acceptable provided both addresses are native to the layer 2 network.

TIP— VIP Host Alias

Make the VIP a host alias!

TIP— VIP Routable Addresses

The pattern where the VIP or VIPs are the only publicly routable address on an Internet-facing appliance works well for scenarios where clients on the Internet connect to DataPower. It offers the advantages of reducing the number of public IP addresses required and of ensuring DataPower cannot contact Internet hosts. However, this pattern does not work if DataPower ever needs to initiate a connection to an Internet host, such as B2B or partner patterns.

━━ ━━ ━━ ━━ ━━ ━━ ━━ ━━ ━━ ━━

Do not enable preemption. As we discussed earlier, it will allow you to have greater certainty about which appliance will be active, but at the cost of more failed transactions. This is the "Two outages for the price of one" configuration button because the first transition, when the Standby becomes Active, was expected and potentially unavoidable. But in the second transition, where the higher-priority takes over for a properly functioning lower-priority appliance, it is not to mitigate anything, it is a takeover for no reason, change only for the sake of change. And it's an expensive change—one that will impact all in-flight transactions.

If there are additional VIPs, they can be added as secondary virtual IP addresses.

━━ ━━ ━━ ━━ ━━ ━━ ━━ ━━ ━━ ━━

TIP— VIP Secondary Host Alias

Make each secondary VIP a host alias!

━━ ━━ ━━ ━━ ━━ ━━ ━━ ━━ ━━ ━━

The priority is the relative rank of group members. The highest priority non-active appliance will be the standby appliance. The net result is that at the point in time when a new Active member is needed, it will be the highest priority appliances of the currently-available group members.

The priority field is the only field that can be different among group members. Every other field must be identical for each member.

Self-balancing can only be enabled if the appliance has the Application Optimization license. If the Application Optimization license is not present, the WebGUI will not show the self-balancing options.

If self-balancing is enabled, the algorithm can be either Round Robin or Weighted Least Connections. We suggest starting with Round Robin.

Weighted least connections tries to keep an appropriate amount of in-flight work associated with each appliance in the group. Under steady state this works well, but when a new member joins it means that a great number of connections all hit the newest member first. Least connections effectively load balances based on when a connection finishes. The weight essentially measures remaining CPU capacity.

Round robin on the other hand distributes incoming connections evenly. It lacks the feedback to slow down on appliances that are completing connections slower, but it does not suffer from the "thundering herd" problem the way weighted least connections does.

No matter which choice you make, you should validate it in a pre-production environment.

The authentication data simply must match on each appliance in the group.

The Hello and Hold timers are defined by HSRP. The Hello timer is the number of seconds between routine HSRP packets. The Hold timer is the amount of time that must pass before advancing state. There should be no reason to change these values except as a debugging technique or as directed by IBM support.

Lastly, we want to point out the "Yield standby" action at the top of the Interface configuration panel. It is not configuration, but it is an important operational control that allows you to gracefully instruct standby control to return to Listen state. When done on an active group member, this causes the Standby group member to immediately become Active. We'll talk more about this when we discuss operations.

Standby control has a status provider that shows each group the appliance is a member of, the primary VIP, the priority, and state. It also shows if self-balancing is enabled and the current distribution algorithm. See Figure 3-4.

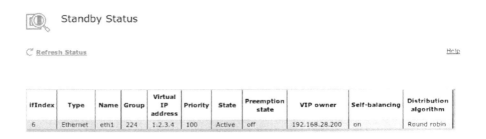

Figure 3-4 Standby Status

The primary status provider for self-balancing is the Self-Balanced Service Status. See Figure 3-5. This is a global status provider showing every self-balanced service for all nodes in the group. It shows the VIP and TCP Port that the client connects to. It shows the IP address of the DataPower appliance that is actually handling the request. It shows information about the DataPower configuration object that produced the service—its domain, type, and name.

"Target state" is Active if the Target IP address is the Active member of the standby control group. In other words, if this field is "Active," then this appliance is the distributor for the VIP. Since the self-balanced service status shows information about all self-balanced standby control groups, the only time you'd see some active and some standby is if the appliance is distributor for one group and not for another.

The Weight, Active Connections, and Inactive Connections columns are special. They are only populated when the appliance is the distributor. Put another way, they are only valid when Target State is Active.

However, since every group member knows how it could forward should it be called upon to perform forwarding, every group member has this table which they would immediately implement if called upon to act as distributor.

Active connections represent the number of established TCP connections the distributor thinks are associated with each appliance. Note that the distributor is only aware of the client to VIP portion of the packet flow, so there can be differences between what the distributor reports and what the target reports in TCP status.

Inactive connections represent the number of connections that have recently been closed. This is roughly similar to the TCP time_wait state for either the client or the target.

Figure 3-5 Self Balanced Service Status

Service Configuration

In order for DataPower services to take advantage of standby control or self-balancing, they simply must use a VIP as their local address or bind address.

Even better is to use a VIP's host-alias as the local address, and use the host-alias as the local address or bind address for the service.

Services with "0.0.0.0" or "::" as the bind address will also take advantage of standby control and self-balancing. However we don't recommended that any service be bound to those addresses when DataPower is connected to more than one security zone. This recommendation holds both with and without standby control.

Standby control is truly transparent to the other services on DataPower. Unlike some other kinds of load balancing, even IP address and TCP port pairs are unchanged.

However, like other kinds of load balancing, each appliance must be truly stateless. There is no guarantee that a client will use the same appliance in a group for multiple requests that make up the same session. Each appliance in the group must be able to handle any connection.

Lastly, load balancing requires enough turnover for it to be effective. Connection reuse is a "Goldilocks" class problem— too much reuse and load balancing isn't effective. Too little reuse and there is significant unnecessary overhead. We're going for just right, as Goldilocks was with the bears' porridge, chair, and bed.

Consider a two-member self-balancing group. The services primarily intra-middleware, and are long-lived HTTPS connections. Now let's say that one of the members goes down, so now all connections are associated with the remaining member.

How can redistribute the load? All the long-lived connections are stuck on the second appliance, and they may never close.

The answer is that we must have some way to limit persistence, to limit connection reuse. For DataPower HTTP and HTTPS Front Side Handlers, the configuration parameter is "Maximum persistent reuse." It should not be set to 0, which is unlimited reuse. See Figure 3-6.

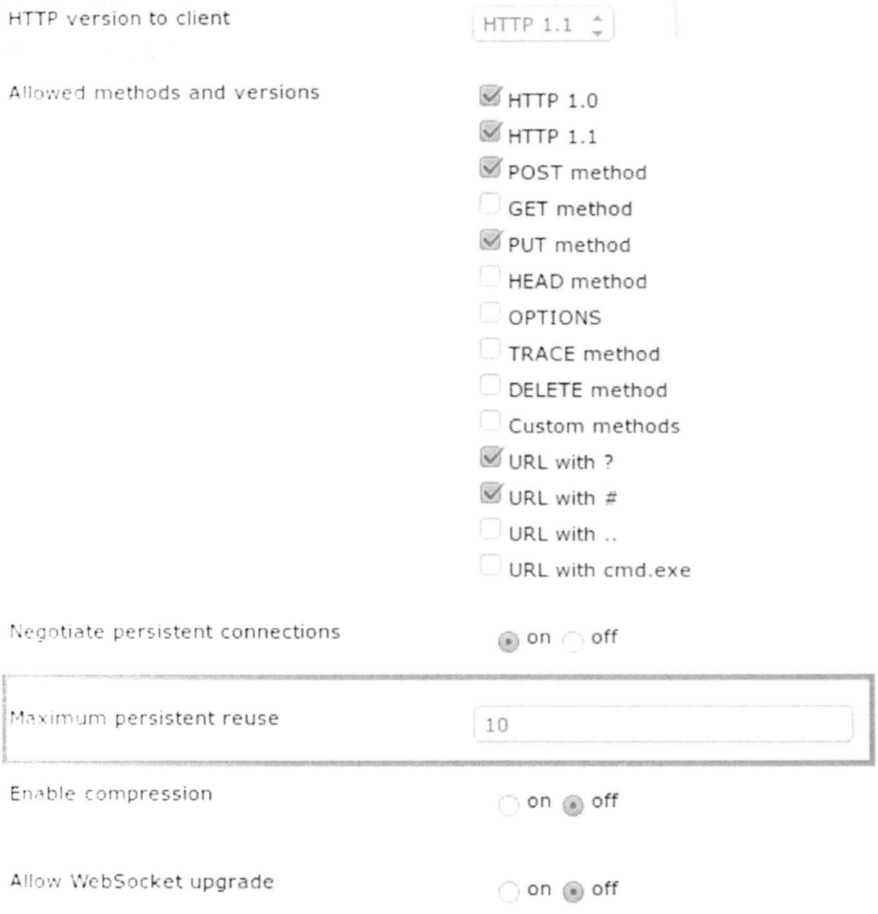

HTTP version to client

HTTP 1.1

Allowed methods and versions

☑ HTTP 1.0
☑ HTTP 1.1
☑ POST method
☐ GET method
☑ PUT method
☐ HEAD method
☐ OPTIONS
☐ TRACE method
☐ DELETE method
☐ Custom methods
☑ URL with ?
☑ URL with #
☐ URL with ..
☐ URL with cmd.exe

Negotiate persistent connections

⦿ on ◯ off

Maximum persistent reuse

10

Enable compression

◯ on ⦿ off

Allow WebSocket upgrade

◯ on ⦿ off

Figure 3-6 HTTP and HTTPS Source Protocol Handler with Maximum Persistent Reuse highlighted

Operations

There are two predominant procedures for performing maintenance on a load-balanced tier of DataPower Gateways.

The first procedure is to use a global load balancer to remove an entire datacenter from production, use the change window to perform maintenance, verify the changes, then use the global load balancer to bring the datacenter back into service. This approach works the same way regardless of the load balancing technology. It is just as applicable to DataPower self-balancing as it is to an external load balancer.

The second procedure is to use the local load balancer to direct traffic away from one node in the local tier, and use the device-specific change window to affect changes before bringing the node back into service.

Standby control without self-balancing does not offer a complete solution for the second procedure. It is not possible to perform a non-destructive controlled takeover from one appliance to another without taking an outage.

However, this can be done with self-balancing. Since DataPower is acting as the local load balancer, we simply need to let the distributor know that it should stop sending connections to the appliance that is under maintenance. Furthermore, we may also need to ensure that the device under maintenance is no longer acting as the distributor. All of this can be done.

The first step is to gracefully direct traffic away from the appliance under maintenance. We do this by quiescing the appliance, domain or service. In this example, we'll consider incrementally updating services and firmware for each appliance in a group, so we'll quiesce the appliance. In the WebGUI Control Panel, Quiesce is available under System Control.

Next we'll monitor the appliance we've quiesced. Watch the TCP status provider and wait until the established connections complete. Latency logs are also helpful to ensure that no transactions are being processed.

Once we have successfully moved all traffic off of the appliance, we want to make sure it's no longer the distributor. Additionally, we'll want to make sure that after the appliance comes back up it does not automatically rejoin the group.

To do this, we can check the standby control status as seen back in Figure 3-4, or we can just yield standby as shown in Figure 3-3.

The yield standby action causes the appliance to go back to Listen state. If this appliance was the distributor, it will no longer be the distributor after the yield. If this appliance was not the distributor, it will no longer be the distributor after the yield.

Now we have an appliance that is not advertising any services due to the quiesce and is not acting as distributor. However, if the appliance were to be rebooted now, it would come back and join the group as a full-fledged member and would once again begin taking connections. This is because the quiesce does not survive a reboot.

It may be that it is acceptable for the appliance to rejoin the group at reboot. If so, the next step is unnecessary.

If we do not want the appliance to rejoin the group at reboot, say because we want to perform some tests on the appliance before it rejoins the group, then we must change the device's configuration. Disabling standby control and saving configuration is sufficient.

At this point, the DataPower appliance has been successfully removed from production. Its services can be upgraded, its firmware changed, it can be powered off and rebooted, secure backup taken, etc. Anything that is contraindicated for a device in production can now be performed safely.

When it is time to bring the device back into production, it can either be rebooted or unquiesced. If the configuration was changed, it can be changed back and saved again.

TIP— Standby Control Setting Persisted

Leaving standby control enabled in the persisted configuration allows proper recovery from abnormal events. If standby control is not enabled in the persisted configuration, and DataPower unexpectedly restarts, the appliance would not rejoin the group until the administrator intervenes.

How to Choose a Local Load Balancer

Deciding what sort of technology to use as a local load balancer is fundamentally a business integration decision.

DataPower's Application Optimization Self-Balancing feature, combined with AO back-end load balancing enhancements makes it a strong candidate when the

DataPower tier is the primary consideration. Its ease of operation is both a blessing and a curse.

Organizations that have business requirements for great granular control over how load balancing is performed may not be satisfied with the level of control self-balancing offers.

Organizations that have well-developed business processes around change windows find it more convenient to use an external load balancer in conjunction with the AO enhancements to back-side load balancing.

The opposite may also be true. Organizations may find it easier to have the single DataPower team in charge of all aspects of the change instead of requiring interlock with other teams, some of which may be external to the organization.

There are a great many factors that must be considered when choosing a local load balancer for any specific deployment. Deciding on the approach that is the best fit for the specific deployment will be a very visible metric by which the success or failure of the project is measured. It is critical to make this decision with eyes wide open.

Summary

Networking is not about how any single node behaves. Networking is about the collective behavior of a broad group of systems, devices, protocols, designs, topologies, concepts, configuration, people, and responsibilities.

Fundamentally, DataPower—like any other node—must integrate properly with "what is" in the broadest sense possible.

The very first integration performed on every DataPower appliance is that with the network. The integration that varies most across the lifecycle of DataPower deployment is the network. It is also probably true that the least understood of all the integrations typically performed with a DataPower appliance is with the network.

We sincerely hope that this volume will help you properly integrate DataPower into your networks at every stage of deployment.

Appendix A: Acronyms Glossary

ACL   Access Control List

ARP   Address Resolution Protocol

BGP   Border Gateway Protocol

BSD   Berkeley Software Distribution

CA   Certificate Authority

CIDR   Classless Inter-Domain Routing

CLI   Command Line Interface

DAC   Direct Attach Copper

DHCP   Dynamic Host Configuration Protocol

DMZ   Demilitarized Zone

DN   Distinguished Name

DNS   Domain Name System

FQDN   Fully Qualified Domain Name

FTP   File Transfer Protocol

HMAC   Hash Message Authentication Code

HTTP   Hypertext Transfer Protocol

HTTPS   Hypertext Transfer Protocol over Secure Socket
Layer

HSRP   Hot Standby Router Protocol

ICAP   Internet Content Adaptation Protocol

ICMP	Internet Control Message Protocol
IDG	IBM DataPower Gateway
IP	Internet Protocol
IPMI	Intelligent Platform Management Interface
LACP	Link Aggregation Control Protocol
LAN	Local Area Network
LDAP	Lightweight Directory Access Protocol
MAC	Media Access Control
MTU	Maximum Transmit Unit
NAT	Network Address Translation
ND	Neighbor Discovery
NFS	Network File System
NTP	Network Time Protocol
OSI	Open Systems Interconnection
OSPF	Open Shortest Path First
RTT	Round Trip Time
SAN	Storage Area Network
SCP	Secure Copy Protocol
SFP+	Small Form-factor Pluggable (enhanced)
SFTP	Secure File Transfer Protocol
SLAAC	Stateless Address Autoconfiguration (for IPv6)
SMTP	Simple Mail Transfer Protocol

SNMP	Simple Network Management Protocol
SSH	Secure Shell
SSL	Secure Sockets Layer
TCP	Transmission Control Protocol
TLS	Transport Layer Security
UDP	User Datagram Protocol
URI	Uniform Resource Identifier
URL	Uniform Resource Locator
VIP	Virtual IP (address)
VLAG	Virtual Link Aggregation
VLAN	Virtual Local Area Network
WML	Wireless Markup Language

Appendix B: DataPower Resources

IBM DataPower Knowledge Center:

http://www-01.ibm.com/support/knowledgecenter/SS9H2Y/welcome

Information Center:

http://www.ibm.com/software/integration/datapower/library/documentation

Internet/WWW Main Product Page:

http://www.ibm.com/datapower

DataPower GitHub:

https://github.com/ibm-datapower

Twitter:

https://twitter.com/IBMGateways

YouTube:

https://www.youtube.com/channel/UCV2_-gdea5LM58S-E3WCqew

LinkedIn:

https://www.linkedin.com/groups?home=&gid=4820454

developerWorks Discussion Forum:

https://www.ibm.com/developerworks/community/forums/html/forum?id=11111111-0000-0000-0000-000000001198

Weekly DataPower Webcast:

https://www14.software.ibm.com/webapp/iwm/web/signup.do?source=swg-wdwfw

SlideShare:

http://www.slideshare.net/ibmdatapower/

How-to find appropriate DataPower product information:

http://www-01.ibm.com/support/docview.wss?uid=swg21377654

DataPower Product Support Website:

Contains firmware, documentation, support procedure, technotes and other helpful material:

http://www.ibm.com/software/integration/datapower/support/

Redbooks:

http://www.redbooks.ibm.com/cgi-bin/searchsite.cgi?query=datapower

Software Services for WebSphere:

Ttop-notch DataPower consulting from IBM WebSphere.

http://www.ibm.com/developerworks/websphere/services/findbykeyword.html?q1=DataPower

Hermann Stamm-Wilbrandt's Blog:

Hermann is one of the brightest minds in DataPower-land, and his blog on development topics is incredibly valuable, featuring tips and techniques that can't be found elsewhere.

https://www.ibm.com/developerworks/community/blogs/HermannSW/?lang=en

WebSphere Global Community DataPower Group:

http://www.websphereusergroup.org/datapower

IBM WebSphere DataPower Support:

http://www.ibm.com/software/integration/datapower/support/

Support Flashes RSS Feed:

http://www-947.ibm.com/systems/support/myfeed/xmlfeeder.wss?feeder.requid=feeder.create_public_feed&feeder.feedtype=RSS&feeder.maxfeed=25&OC=SS9H2Y&feeder.subdefkey=swgws&feeder.channel.title=WebSphere%20DataPower%20SOA%20Appliances&feeder.channel.descr=The%20latest%20updates%20about%20WebSphere%20DataPower%20SOA%20Appliances

IBM DataPower Support Technotes:

http://www.ibm.com/search/csass/search?q=&sn=spe&lang=en&filter=collection:stgsysx,dblue,ic,pubs,devrel1&prod=U692969C82819Q63

IBM Education Assistant DataPower Modules:

http://www-01.ibm.com/support/knowledgecenter/websphere_iea/com.ibm.iea.wdatapower/plugin_coverpage.dita

WAMC Technote:

http://www-01.ibm.com/support/docview.wss?uid=swg24032265

DataPower Feature Grid:

We consider the Feature Grid to be an invaluable resource, and we are excited to provide it to you. It yields the answers to the most commonly asked questions about DataPower ("Is feature/protocol/spec X supported on my Y appliance?") We had initially included the entire table here, spread across several pages. However, due to its density, it was hard to read, and it was literally changing under us as product management made changes for the impending announcements.

We debated and felt that the best thing we could do for our readers would be to provide a URL hyperlink, so that the most up to date information (and not stale or incorrect information!) is available to you. There are detriments to this approach, such as the dreaded 'busted URL', but in this day and age it's likely that you are reading this on a device with an Internet connection, or have one within reach, and as well we have the capability to update this book as soon as we find that something is amiss. You can find the features grid at:

http://www.slideshare.net/ibmdatapower/ibm-data-power-gateways-features-comparison

Acknowledgements

The Author Team:

We thank the IBM management team for allowing us to access the resources necessary to write the book.

The author team would like to thank Colt Gustafson for his technical review, and the following people for technical contributions, clarifications, and suggestions for this book: Jaime Ryan (first edition co-author), Arif Siddiqui (including updates to the performance info), Bhargav Perepa, Chris Cross, Shiu-Fun Poon, Russell Butek, Trey Williamson, Colt Gustafson, David Maze, David Shute, Eugene Kuznetsov, Gari Singh, Greg Truty, Henry Chung, Joel Smith, John de Frietas, John Graham, Julie Salamone, Ken Hygh, Keys Botzum, Rich Groot, Marcel Kinard, Rich Salz, Steve Hanson, Tom Alcott, Naipaul Ojar, Davin Holmes, Jon Harry, and Paul Glezen.

Bill Hines:

I'd like to thank Keys Botzum and Kyle Brown for being role models for work ethic and integrity, and mentoring me throughout my IBM career. I'd like to thank my immediate and extended family for being supportive and understanding during the tough times. Last, I'd like to thank my author team for sticking with this project during the many months, nights, and weekends of heated debates and stress. You were all picked for a reason, and I think the fact that you have all put up with me, and we have been through what we have and emerged still good friends with tremendous respect for each other, attests to those decisions being good ones. I'm extremely proud of the job you've done.

John Rasmussen:

I was lucky enough to have joined DataPower during its initial startup phase, and to have worked with some truly talented and inspirational people through its acquisition by IBM. The list is too long, but I'd like to thank Eugene Kuznetsov for making this all possible and for providing me with the opportunity to participate, Rich Salz for his generosity of time and knowledge and the many contributions he made to DataPower, Brian Del Vecchio for making building the WebGUI fun. And the many individuals who I came to respect and to rely on in tough times including; Jan-Christian Nelson, Gari Singh, David Maze, John Shriver, Tony Ffrench, James Ricotta, Shiu-Fun Poon and many others within and beyond the DataPower and IBM families. To my fellow authors, with a special word of appreciation to Bill Hines, as there is no doubt that without Bill's tremendous effort and continuous dedication these books would not have happened.

Harley Stenzel:

Thanks to the author team for inviting me to join for the second edition of the DataPower Handbook, it's been a great experience. In addition to the many DataPower folks already mentioned, I'd like to thank Adolfo Rodriguez for his trusted council, Srinivasan Muralidharan and Bob Callaway for showing me the DataPower ropes. Also thanks to Tim Smith and Tony Wrobel for being gracious despite being unlucky enough to face many of my questions. The wider DataPower team, my colleagues, many of you have helped me in ways big and small. Thank you.

Jim Brennan:

I would like to thank all of my co-authors for including me in the writing of this book and for making it the best that it could be. I would especially like to thank Bill Hines for getting the band back together to get the latest information out there in this, and future volumes. I would like to thank my family and friends for being understanding and supportive when the stress seemed to be getting the best of me.

Ozair Sheikh:

I would like to thank my co-authors for giving me the opportunity to contribute to this book. A special thanks to Bill Hines whose hard work and leadership made this book a reality. I have been fortunate to work with a talented group of people during my career. Special thanks to my managers who recognized my contributions and provided me with opportunities to grow. I would also like to thank my IBM colleagues, Arif Siddiqui, Robert Conti, Ken Hygh, Tony Ffrench, Shiu-Fun Poon, Rachel Reinitz, Salman Moghul and Fred Tucci. I would like to thank my family and friends for supporting me in reaching my career goals.

About the Authors

Bill Hines

Bill is an IBM Executive I/T Specialist. His current role is as WebSphere Federal Chief Technical Architect and Strategist, working out of Lake Hopatcong, NJ. He has many years of IBM WebSphere solution design and implementation experience in both customer engagements and developing and delivering internal training within IBM. He is the lead author of the acclaimed IBM Press book IBM WebSphere DataPower SOA Appliance Handbook (first and second editions) and co-author of IBM WebSphere: Deployment and Advanced Configuration, as well as many articles published in WebSphere Technical Journal and developerWorks.

John Rasmussen

John is a Senior Engineer within the IBM DataPower organization. John has been with IBM and DataPower since 2001 and has worked as a product development engineer (where he created and developed the original WebGUI Drag and Drop Policy Editor) and as a product specialist assisting many clients in the implementation of DataPower devices. John has an extensive career in software development, including work with McCormack & Dodge/D&B Software, Fidelity Investments and as an independent consultant. John has a degree from the University of Massachusetts at Amherst, and lives in Gloucester, Massachusetts.

Harley Stenzel

Harley is a Senior Engineer within the IBM DataPower development organization, where he is the networking subject matter expert. His career spans wide swath of enterprise networking, ranging from load balancers to firewalls to cross-platform kernel network development. Harley's notable DataPower projects include self-balancing, link aggregation and cloud integration. Normally Harley is found behind the scenes, but he is often called in for difficult business problems that have a significant network component. Harley holds degrees from Ohio University in Applied Mathematics and Computer Science and lives in Hillsborough, North Carolina.

Jim Brennan

Jim is a partner and president of an independent consulting firm, McIndi Solutions. McIndi Solutions is an IBM business partner based out of Hackettstown, NJ specializing in DataPower administration and configuration. Jim has assisted in developing and delivering internal DataPower education material to IBM consultants and engineers. Jim has also been an application developer working with several different programming languages and platforms ranging from COBOL to

Java. Jim has been a JEE developer for several years specializing in JEE development for WebSphere Application Server. He also has several years of experience with WebSphere Application Server installation, configuration, troubleshooting, and administration. Jim has more than ten years of I/T experience with a certificate from the Chubb Institute of Technology and also attended Felician College in Lodi, NJ.

Ozair Sheikh

Ozair is a Senior Product Line Manager for IBM DataPower Gateways and certified IBM IT Specialist. He is an experienced SOA/ESB/Mobile IT professional with over 10 years in managing, consulting, instructing and developing enterprise solutions using WebSphere technologies. He is avid speaker at several worldwide conferences; topics ranging from Mobile security, API Management and architecting mission-critical ESB systems.

In his current role, Ozair helps drive new innovative solutions for the DataPower gateway platform that reflect customer requirements and market trends. Ozair holds a bachelor of Mathematics with specialization in Computer Science from the University of Waterloo. In his spare time, he is an avid hockey and basketball fan, and enjoys writing mobile apps to solve his everyday problems.

Afterword

Afterword by Eugene Kuznetsov

"The proper planning of any job is the first requirement. With limited knowledge of a trade, the job of planning is doubly hard, but there are certain steps that any person can take towards proper planning if he only will."

—Robert Oakes Jordan, Masonry

I founded a company called DataPower® in the spring of 1999 to build products based on several distinct ideas. The first idea involved applying reconfigurable computing and dynamic code generation to the problem of integrating disparate applications. The second idea centered on the concept of data-oriented programming (DOP) as the means to achieve direct and robust data interchange. The third idea involved delivering middleware as a network function, enabled by the DOP technology and inspired by the successful models of ubiquitous connectivity. The product's journey since has been remarkable, and this great book is another milestone for the entire team behind DataPower. Before more discussion of the book itself, a few words on these three ideas.

Rapidly adapting to change is key for everything and everyone in today's world, and IBM appliances are no exception. Whether it's a policy, a transformation map, a schema, or a security rule, DataPower will try to put it into effect with as little delay and interruption as possible. Popular methods for maintaining this kind of flexibility come with a large performance penalty. However, by dynamically generating code and reconfiguring hardware based on the current message flow, it became possible to achieve both flexibility and near-optimal performance. At any given point, the device operates as a custom engine for a particular task, but when the task changes, it can rapidly become a different custom engine underneath the covers.

This dynamic adaptability is especially useful when combined with DOP. Stated briefly, DOP emphasizes formally documenting data formats and using them directly, instead of encapsulation or abstraction, to integrate or secure different modules or systems. Today, XML is probably one of the most successful and readily recognized examples of DOP, but the principles are more universal than any particular technology. Another example of DOP is the way DataPower XI52 processes binary data, by using high-level format descriptors instead of adaptors.

These, in turn, enable the creation of network hardware (also known as appliance) products that operate on whole application messages (rather than network packets) to integrate, secure, or control applications. Greater simplicity, performance, security, and cost-effectiveness were envisioned—and are now proven—with the appliance approach. Beyond the appliance design discipline, the success of IP & Ethernet networking in achieving universal connectivity has much to teach about the best way to achieve radically simplified and near-universal application integration.

Reading this book will enable you to benefit from the previous three ideas in their concrete form: the award-winning IBM products they became. From basic setup to the most powerful advanced features, it covers DataPower appliances in a readable tone with a solid balance of theory and examples. For example, Chapter 6 does a great job in explaining the big-picture view of device operation, and Chapter 22 gives a detailed how-to on extending its capabilities. With some of the most experienced hands-on DataPower practitioners among its authors, it provides the kind of real-world advice that is essential to learning any craft.

When learning IBM DataPower, there is one thing that may be more helpful and rewarding than remembering every particular detail, and that is developing an internal "mental model" of how the devices are meant to operate and fit into the environment. Especially when troubleshooting or learning new features, this "mental model" can make device behavior intuitive. Reading the following pages with an eye toward not just the details but also this mental model will speed both productivity and enjoyment.

In conclusion, I would like to use this occasion to thank the entire team, past and present, who made and continues to make DataPower possible. Their work and the passion of DataPower users is an inspiring example of how great people and a powerful idea can change the world for the better.

—*Eugene Kuznetsov, Cambridge, MA Founder of DataPower Technology, Inc. served as President, Chairman, and CTO at various points in the company's history, and then served as director of Product Management and Marketing, SOA Appliances at IBM Corporation.*

DataPower's first office is on the right. Photo courtesy of Merryman Design.

Afterword by Jerry Cuomo

It all started when I was asked to co-host an IBM Academy Conference on "Accelerators and Off-Loading" in 2004. I was feeling a little out of my element, so I decided to take some of the focus off me and put it on others. I had been reading about some of the new XML-centered hardware devices and was intrigued. I have always been interested in system performance. With XML dominating our emerging workloads (e.g., Service Oriented Architecture), the impact of XML performance on system performance was becoming increasingly important. Hence, I thought it would be a good idea to invite a handful of these XML vendors to our conference.

At the conference, the DataPower presentation was quite different from the others. It wasn't about ASICs or transistors; it was about improving time to value and total cost of operation. The DataPower presentation focused on topics that were also near and dear to me, such as systems integration, configuration over programming, and the merits of built-for-purpose systems. In essence, Eugene Kuznetsov, the DataPower founder and presenter, was talking about the value of appliances. While very intriguing, I couldn't help but feel curious about whether the claims were accurate. So, after the conference I invited Eugene to come to our lab in Research Triangle Park in North Carolina to run some tests.

I have to admit now that in the back of my mind, I operated on the principle of "keeping your friends close and your enemies closer." Behind my intrigue was a feeling of wanting to understand their capabilities so that we could outperform vendors with WebSphere® Application Server. The tests went well; however, the DataPower team was somewhat reluctant to dwell on the raw XML performance capabilities of their appliance. Feeling a little suspicious, I had my team run some raw performance experiments. The results were off the charts. Why wasn't the DataPower team flaunting this capability? This is when I had my "ah-ha" moment. While performance measured in transactions per second is important and part of the value equation, the overall performance metrics found while assessing time to value and overall cost of operation and ownership are the most critical performance metrics to a business. This is where the DataPower appliances outperform. I read a paper, written by Jim Barton, CTO and co-founder of Tivo, called "Tivo-lution." The paper was inspiring as it confirmed the motivations and aspirations that I've had ever since I led IBM's acquisition of DataPower in 2005. In the paper, Barton describes the challenges of making complex systems usable and how "purpose-built" computer systems are one answer to the challenge:

"One of the greatest challenges of designing a computer system is in making sure the system itself is 'invisible' to the user. The system should simply be a conduit to the desired result. There are many examples of such purpose-built systems, ranging from modern automobiles to mobile phones."

The concept of purpose-built systems is deeply engrained in our DNA at IBM. The name of our company implies this concept: International Business Machines.

IBM has a long history of building purposed machines, such as the 1933 Type 285, an electric bookkeeping and accounting machine. I can imagine this machine being delivered to an accountant, plugging it in, immediately followed by number crunching. The accountant didn't have to worry about hard drive capacity, operating system levels, compatibility between middleware vendors, or application functionality. It just did the job. I can also imagine it followed the 80/20 rule. It probably didn't do 100% of what all accountants needed. But it probably did 80% of what all accountants needed very well. Users just dealt with the remaining 20%, or learned to live without it.

"Business Machines, Again" is my inspiration. Our customers respond positively to the re-emergence of this approach to engineering products. It's all about time-to-value and total cost of operation and ownership. Appliances such as our WebSphere DataPower are leading the way in delivering on these attributes.

At the extreme, purpose-built systems, such as a Tivo DVR and an XI52, are built from the ground up for their purposes. While they might use off-the-shelf parts, such as an embedded Linux® OS, it is important that all parts are "right sized" for the job. Right-sizing source code in a hardware appliance is more like firmware (with strong affinity to the underlying hardware) than it is software. As such, the Tivo-lution paper describes the need to own every line of source code to ensure the highest level of integration and quality:

"...by having control of each and every line of source code...

Tivo would have full control of product quality and development schedules. When the big bug hunt occurred, as it always does, we needed the ability to follow every lead, understand every path, and track every problem down to its source."

The Tivo team even modified the GNU C++ compiler to eliminate the use of exceptions (which generate a lot of code that is seldom used) in favor of rigid checking of return code usage in the firmware. DataPower similarly contains a custom XML compiler that generates standard executable code for its general-purpose CPUs, as well as custom code for the (XG4) XML coprocessor card.

A physical appliance has the unparalleled benefit of being hardened for security. Jim talks about this in his Tivo paper:

"Security must be fundamental to the design...We wanted to make it as difficult as possible, within the economics of the DVR platform, to corrupt the security of any particular DVR."

The DataPower team has taught me the meaning of "tamper-proof" appliances, or more precisely "tamper-evident." Like the 1982 Tylenol scare, we can't stop you from opening the box, but we can protect you, if someone does open it. In fact, the physical security characteristics of DataPower make it one of the only technologies some of our most stringent customers will put on their network Demilitarized Zone (DMZ). If a DataPower box is compromised and opened, it basically stops working. An encrypted flash drive makes any configuration data, including security keys, difficult to exploit. "DP is like the roach motel; private keys go in, but never come out" is the way we sometimes describe the tamper-proof qualities of DataPower.

But the truth is, DataPower is not a DVR. DataPower is a middleware appliance. Middleware is a tricky thing to make an appliance out of. Middleware is enabling technology and by its nature is not specific to any application or vendor. The Tivo appliance is a specific application (TV and guide) that makes it somewhat easier to constrain:

"Remember, it's television. Everybody knows how television works."

"Television never stops, even when you turn off the TV set. Televisions never crash."

Hence, the challenge (and the art) in building a middleware appliance involves providing the right amount of constraint, without rendering the appliance useless. For example, DataPower does not run Java™ code (which is the primary means of customizing much of the WebSphere portfolio); instead, it uses XML as the primary mode of behavior customization. So, at some level, DP is not programmed, but instead it is configured. Now, for those who have used XML (and its cousin XSLT), you know that it's more than configuration; however, it is a constraint over Java programming, which has unbounded levels of customizability. The combined team of IBM and DataPower have been bridging this gap (of special to general purpose) effectively. We have recently added features to DP to allow it to seamlessly connect to IBM mainframe software (IMS™ and DB2®) as well as capabilities to manage a collection of appliances as if they were one.

IBM has a healthy general-purpose software business. Our WebSphere, Java-based middleware is the poster child for general-purpose middleware (write once, run almost everywhere). However, there is a place for business machines that are purposed built and focus on providing the 80 part of the 80/20 rule. We are heading down this path in a Big Blue way.

This book represents an important milestone in the adoption of DataPower into the IBM family. The authors of this book represent some of IBM's most skilled practitioners of Service Oriented Architecture (SOA). This team is a customer facing team and has a great deal of experience in helping our customers quickly realize value from our products. They have also been among the most passionate within IBM of adopting the appliance approach to rapidly illustrating the value of SOA to our customers. The authors have unparalleled experience in using DataPower to solve some of our customers' most stringent systems integration problems. This book captures their experiences and best practices and is a valuable tool for deriving the most out of your WebSphere DataPower appliance.

—Jerry Cuomo, IBM Fellow, WebSphere CTO

Afterword by Kyle Brown

I can still remember the day in late 2005 when Jerry Cuomo first called me into his office to tell me about an acquisition (then pending) of a small Massachusetts company that manufactured hardware devices.

"Wait a minute. Hardware??!?"

That's the first incredulous thought that went through my mind. Jerry was the CTO of the WebSphere brand in IBM, which had become the industry-leading brand of middleware based on Java. Why were we looking at a company that made hardware? Echoing the immortal words of Dr. "Bones" McCoy from the classic Star Trek series, I then thought,

"I'm a software engineer, not a hardware engineer, dang it!"

But as I sat in his office, Jerry wove me a story (as he had for our executives) that soon had me convinced that this acquisition did, in fact, make sense for WebSphere as a brand and for IBM as a whole. Jerry had the vision of a whole new way of looking at SOA middleware—a vision that encompassed efficient, special-purpose appliances that could be used to build many of the parts of an SOA. Key to this vision was the acquisition of DataPower, which gave us not only a wealth of smart people with deep experience in Networking, XML, and SOA, but an entry into this field with the DataPower family of appliances—notably the Integration appliance.

Since that day, I've never regretted our decision to branch out the WebSphere brand well beyond its Java roots. The market response to the introduction of the DataPower appliances to the brand has been nothing short of phenomenal. Far from distracting us, the ability to provide our customers with an easy-to-use, easy-to-install, and remarkably efficient hardware-based option for their ESB and security needs has turned out to be an asset that created synergy with our other product lines and made the brand stronger as a whole. It's been an incredible journey, and as we begin to bring out new appliances in the DataPower line, we're only now beginning to see the fundamental shift in thinking that appliance-based approaches can give us.

On this journey, I've been accompanied by a fantastic group of people—some who came to us through the DataPower acquisition and some who were already part of the WebSphere family—who have helped our customers make use of these new technologies. Bill, John, and the rest of the author team are the true experts in this technology, and their expertise and experience show in this book.

This book provides a wealth of practical information for people who are either novices with the DataPower appliances, or who want to learn how to get the most from their appliances. It provides comprehensive coverage of all the topics that are necessary to master the DataPower appliance, from basic networking and security concepts, through advanced configuration of the Appliance's features. It provides copious, detailed examples of how the features of the appliances work, and provides debugging help and tips for helping you determine how to make those examples (and your own projects) work. But what's most helpful about this book is the way in which the team has given you not just an explanation of how you would use each feature, but also why the features are built the way they are. Understanding the thinking behind the approaches taken is an enormous help in fully mastering these appliances. The team provides that, and provides you with a wealth of hints, tips, and time-saving advice not just for using and configuring devices, but also for how to structure your work with the devices.

This book is something the DataPower community has needed for a long time, and I'm glad that the authors have now provided it to the community. So sit back, crack open the book, open up the admin console (unless you have yet to take the appliance out of the box—the book will help you there, too!) and begin. Your work with the appliances is about to get a whole lot easier, more comprehensible, and enjoyable as well.

—*Kyle Brown, Distinguished Engineer, IBM Software Services and Support*

CPSIA information can be obtained at www.ICGtesting.com
Printed in the USA
BVOW02s1053240116

434044BV00022B/648/P